Rob Woolmington

JAMAICA KINCAID

TALK STORIES

Jamaica Kincaid was born in St. John's, Antigua. Her books include *At the Bottom of the River, Annie John, Lucy, The Autobiography of My Mother, Mr. Potter, My Brother*, and *See Now Then*. She lives in Vermont.

ALSO BY JAMAICA KINCAID

TALK
STORIES

Foreword by Ian Frazier

Picador

Farrar, Straus and Giroux

New York

TALK
STORIES

JAMAICA
KINCAID

Picador

120 Broadway, New York 10271

Printed in the United States of America

Originally published in 2001 by Farrar, Straus and Giroux

First paperback edition, 2002

Paperback reissue edition, 2024

These works, with the exception of Ian Frazier's foreword
and Jamaica Kincaid's introduction, first appeared in
The New Yorker. Grateful acknowledgment is made to George
Trow for permission to reprint "West Indian Weekend."

The Library of Congress has cataloged the Farrar, Straus and Giroux
hardcover edition as follows:

Kincaid, Jamaica.

   Talk Stories / Jamaica Kincaid.

     p. cm.

   ISBN 13: 978-0-374-27239-5

   I. Title.

PR9275.A583 K56385 2000   00-042684

2024 Paperback ISBN: 978-1-250-34062-7

Designed by Jonathan D. Lippincott

Our books may be purchased in bulk for promotional,
educational, or business use. Please contact your local bookseller
or the Macmillan Corporate and Premium Sales Department
at 1-800-221-7945, extension 5442, or by email at
MacmillanSpecialMarkets@macmillan.com.

Picador® is a U.S. registered trademark and is used by Macmillan
Publishing Group, LLC, under license from Pan Books Limited.

For book club information, please email marketing@picadorusa.com.

picadorusa.com • Follow us on social media at @picador or @picadorusa

1 3 5 7 9   10 8 6 4 2

For George Trow and for Sandy Frazier

Contents

Foreword

⚜

This is a story I always tell about Jamaica:

When she and I were staff writers at *The New Yorker* magazine with offices across the hall from each other—twenty-five years ago—we often had dinner together at the end of the day. We would leave work on the late side, after the office was mostly empty and rush hour had eased, and walk or take the subway from Forty-third Street in Manhattan, where *The New Yorker* was, to Jamaica's apartment on West Twenty-second. Often we stopped at a store along the way and bought something to cook. Then I would sit in her apartment and drink three or four beers while she made dinner, and then we would eat at a small table while watching TV shows like *Andy of Mayberry* or *Mary Hartman, Mary Hartman* or the miniseries *Roots*. After dinner we would talk for a while, and then I would go home.

Sometimes on the way to her apartment we would buy our dinner at a store called the Chelsea Charcuterie. This was a little gourmet-food store on Ninth Avenue near her place. Nowadays you can get gourmet items such as cilantro or curried chicken salad at the A&P, but back then gourmet shops like the Chelsea Charcuterie existed hardly anywhere; this store was an early hint of the gourmet-food explosion that was to come. The owners of the store were about our age and they liked Jamaica and let her run a tab. Once, she told me she owed them over eight hundred dollars, an amount so large I could not imagine how it could ever be paid off. Jamaica usually talked to Francie, one of the owners, for a long time while she decided on what to buy. One evening she was shopping, and she and Francie were chatting, when a guy with a loud boom-box radio came in and asked for change for a twenty. In high-minded irritation Jamaica turned to him and said, "You know, this isn't the kind of store where you can just walk in and ask for change for a twenty." I remember the guy as little, skinny, and pointy, with an aerodynamically shaped face that looked as if you could throw it and it would make a big circle in the air and end up at your feet. The guy turned to Jamaica and said, furiously and matter-of-factly, "Lady, I'm going to go home, get my gun, come back here, and blow you away." Then he walked quickly out of the store.

I had arrived in New York at the age of twenty-three with the idea of becoming a writer. I was always keyed up and scared and full of expectations then, and sometimes I met people who were like no one I had ever met before, people who did amazing things. This moment in the Chelsea Charcuterie was a height of amazement for me. Just about everybody I had ever known, including me, would have left the store right away. Shootings used to happen in New York all the time back then. There had been a shooting not far from that store, and I had seen the victim's bright red blood on the sidewalk. After the pointy guy left, however, Jamaica merely continued to shop. Her consideration of the items which would be tastiest for our dinner became, if anything, even more leisurely and serene. I desperately wanted to get out of there, but of course I couldn't show my fear, not in front of a girl. And I couldn't just run away—that would have been un-gallant. Silently I accepted that in a few minutes my friend and I would be dead, and I regarded the items in the store in a mood of self-pitying farewell; I remember in particular a low barrel of rough blond wood filled with Ghanaian coffee beans.

A lot of the exhilaration of those years for me was in see-ing who could be the bravest, who could be the coolest. I kept a mental scorecard of brave and cool deeds: I saw young *New Yorker* veterans George Trow and Tony Hiss come into the of-fice an hour or two before an issue's deadline and in one draft turn out Talk of the Town stories as elegant and effortless as a Will Rogers rope trick. I saw a guy climb the outside of the World Trade Center, 110 stories tall. I saw the comedian Richard Pryor performing live in concert at the Felt Forum when he made the audience laugh so hard that laughter be-came a painful spasm they couldn't control. I saw a city meter maid hurry over to a fallen-down street person I wouldn't have touched with gloves on and gently cradle his head in her lap until an ambulance arrived. I saw the actor John Belushi deflect the aggressive attentions of a drunken fan who should have been in custody and do it in a way that turned the encounter into a playful exercise in theater. But to me, nobody was braver than Jamaica. She didn't try to be shocking or "transgressive" or audacious, those imitations of bravery done mainly for effect; her bravery was just the way she was, and it came natural and uninterrupted from inside.

Once, at some fancy New York function, she met and talked to Jacqueline Onassis, and shortly after, at another function happened to be introduced to her again. Jacqueline Onassis greeted Jamaica the second time without any sign of recognition; Jamaica said to her, "We've met," and walked away. Once in a movie theater a thuggish guy was talking loudly behind us and Jamaica asked him to be quiet and he cursed at her and said if she didn't turn around and shut up he would cut her face; she gave him a few choice words and went back to watching the movie. I took her trout fishing in a deep and fast river in Vermont and she waded in after me in jeans and sneakers; only later I found out that she didn't know how to swim. She and I used to go up to Harlem sometimes to visit a woman she knew on 128th Street or to see shows at the Apollo Theatre. This was back in the days of Black Power and honky-go-home, and people almost always made remarks to us. A lady in a hat called Jamaica a "black concubine," lots of guys speculated about us loudly and obscenely. Whatever rudeness people said, Jamaica would agree with in the polite and helpful manner of a first-grade teacher: "Yes, you're right, I am [whatever]." "Yes, that's true, I do [whatever]." Once, some guys harassed us from the windows of a prison bus and she yelled back that at least she wasn't a criminal going off to jail.

Then there was the pajama phase. I can't leave that out. Once, she spent several days in Sloan-Kettering, a cancer hospital in Manhattan, for surgery that could have been serious but luckily wasn't, and while she was there she fell in love with the pajamas the hospital issued to her. These pajamas were of a crepe-like seersucker, blue-and-white striped, with matching knee-length bathrobe and paper slippers. She liked the pajamas so much that after she got out of the hospital she wore them everywhere. I would show up at her apartment— she was living downtown then, in SoHo—to escort her to a movie or a *New Yorker* event uptown, and she would come to the door in pajamas, robe, and paper slippers. I have no fashion sense at all, so I held my tongue, but I almost expressed an opinion that wearing pajamas for evening attire makes you look kind of insane. I knew she would wear them regardless of what I said. The time of year was spring, so at least her clothing was not unseasonable. Getting a cab in Manhattan is often difficult, but I learned that when you are accompanied by a six-foot-tall black woman in pajamas, it is more difficult still.

For us, the whole point was the writing. Each bold deed we saw or did was like a sketch of what a good piece of writing should be; we were just learning how to write, but somehow we knew that fearlessness was key. It sounds melodramatic to say that we believed we must write or die, but then youth itself is melodramatic. Our opinions about ourselves and other writers were merciless and extreme. Jamaica believed that one's writing should always come first, before one's personal life, and when she was twenty-five she made me promise that if she ever got married and had children I must take her aside and tell her she was no longer a writer. (Of course, she has now been married for many years and has two children, the older one a teenager.) This youthful fierceness of purpose Jamaica directed toward writing short nonfiction pieces for the Talk of the Town department of *The New Yorker*, and in particular for the man who was the magazine's editor, William Shawn. Each Talk story she wrote back then was a jump further into writing, a new exploration of her voice within the magazine's discipline of subject matter and form. In a sense, the record of Jamaica's becoming a writer is the collection of her Talk pieces assembled here.

The first piece of hers the magazine published was a report she did (at the urging of George Trow, and with a short introduction by him) on the subject of a West Indian Day parade in Brooklyn. Jamaica's account stood out three-dimensionally from the text around it like a combination of regular print and Braille, giving notice of a new voice in the magazine and a major writer on the way. Later she said that in doing that piece she understood for the first time that writing wasn't something outside her but just her thoughts inside her head. Oddly, her first Talk piece was also the only one in which her name appeared; the items in the department were almost all anonymous back then. From that beginning she went on to write pieces about concerts, promotional parties, people famous at the time, and an unexpected and moving description of a convention of New York City police detectives in which the loud plaidness of their suitcoats was a recurring theme. Some of her pieces were parodies of Nancy Drew–type adventure fiction for girls, others were dialogues between made-up characters in which the actual event being described emerged only in shattered, cubistic form. Some of her pieces were witty cries of frustration at the magazine's sometimes suffocating proprieties.

You couldn't use curse words, or dirty words, or write about sex in Talk of the Town. You couldn't write about religion. You couldn't write about the journalistic topic of the week, the one every reporter at every other publication was writing about, unless you did it in a completely different way. You couldn't be too mean. Stories involving violence or blood sports were out; ditto anything that was overly commercial or boosterish or had been done too recently before. Also, what you wrote should be about or take place in New York City; this was *The New Yorker*, after all. Mr. Shawn did not state his taboos and restrictions explicitly—and all these were his, no question—but you learned them through the painful rejection of submitted ideas and through stories that were written and handed in and never heard from again.

And yet aside from that, amazingly, you were pretty much free. Within certain boundaries—which could even be crossed if you had luck and knew how—you could write about anything you liked in any way you liked. It's hard to imagine a major magazine today being so self-willed and heedless of convention in its editorial policy, harder still to imagine such a policy succeeding as *The New Yorker*'s did. For Jamaica, the discipline was a challenge and the freedom heady. One week she decided to submit as her Talk story a list of the expenses incurred in reporting the story. Another week she wrote a long, introspective letter in the first person describing a train trip she had taken to New York from Cleveland. Another week she went into detail about a Thanksgiving dinner she had just made which copied to the cranberry a recent Thanksgiving dinner of a Midwestern family as described in a women's magazine. As her Talk stories grew more adventuresome and complex and skilled, the fictional pieces which would make her famous began to appear in the magazine. Her Talk stories also served as experimental warm-ups for her much-anthologized fiction works like "Girl," "At the Bottom of the River," and "In the Night."

If the inventiveness and determination in her Talk stories were Jamaica's alone, the editorial ear was Mr. Shawn's. This collection can also be seen as the account of an apprenticeship, or as an unfolding conversation between a young writer and a man who had been editing Talk stories since well before she was born. Adding dimension to their relationship was the fact that a few years after Jamaica made me promise to tell her she was no longer a writer if she married, she met and married Mr. Shawn's son Allen. (A composer and teacher of music theory, Allen has gotten to know his wife's outspokenness well; his reply, after a particularly frank comment of hers: "Dear, please! Mince words!") Recently people have written a lot about Mr. Shawn's strengths and weaknesses as an editor and a human being. Usually everybody agrees that he was perhaps the greatest editor of his day, without offering many specific examples of his editorial skill. This collection, with its invisible plot of a unique new writer being allowed a freedom to emerge story by story, is evidence also of a great editor doing his job.

For readers familiar with Jamaica's fiction, these pieces will give an idea of what she was like when she was young and just starting out. Some may recognize pieces they remember but hadn't realized were hers. In virtually all the pieces, stylistic elements which would reappear in her fictional works can be seen in nascent form; other flourishes of style found here were once-only performances done just for the heck of it and left forever behind. Unlike many Talk pieces, and unlike almost all writing in magazines, these pieces published originally with no signature turn out now to be unmistakably *by* a specific person—they're completely cast in Jamaica's voice, and filled with her sensibility.

Some of them I remember seeing for the first time in her typewriter, half-done. I used to go across the hall to Jamaica's office and read what she was writing and rush back to my office in a fever of literary desire. I sometimes wished the story in my typewriter were hers, and I imagined copying hers, or just taking it by subterfuge: "Good job, Kincaid—no need to stay around—I'll just finish this up for you and see that it gets to Mr. Shawn!" Watching a piece of hers emerge out of empty air gave to writing a live-action vividness that words on paper don't usually have. In my saner and less covetous moments, I used my envy as inspiration to try and write something myself, happy just to be playing on the same field.

Usually we were broke or almost broke in our Talk-writing days, but after reading Jamaica, or even after talking to her, I often felt suddenly wealthy, as if I had just remembered a large and long-forgotten bank account in my name. I think this book will make other readers feel the same. Her writing is a shared plenitude, a promise of more where that came from. In these early pieces, as in all her work, Jamaica Kincaid appears as a writer of boldness and encouragement who keeps on showing us the ever-dawning possibilities in writing and in the world.

—Ian Frazier

TALK
STORIES

Introduction

All sentences, all paragraphs about this part of my life, my life as a writer, must begin with George Trow. It is possible that he will not like this, but it is the truth all the same, I must begin with George Trow.

When I was young I wanted to write and I did not know how to do that, write, and I didn't even know how it was done, but I wanted to do it all the same, and so I used to go around and tell everyone who asked me what I did, that I was a writer and if I was not yet a writer, I wanted to be one all the same. At one minute I wanted to be a writer, and instinctively realizing I was in America, the next minute I decided I was a writer, and so when anyone asked me who I was, I said, I am a writer. I did not know exactly what that means, I still do not know exactly what that means, but even now, when I am asked what it is that I am, I say, I am a writer.

It was as a writer that I applied to a magazine called then, and still called even now, *Mademoiselle*, for a job as a writer,

and they said no, and when I told my friends or anyone else
that I had applied for a job at that magazine (called *Mademoiselle* then and still called that now) and was turned down,
they said to me that a magazine like that, *Mademoiselle*,
would not hire black girls. How stupid of them, *Mademoiselle*,
I thought, for I had grown up in a place where quite a few
people I knew had been girls and many, many, many more
than that had been black, and so I paid no attention to *Mademoiselle* then and even less than that now. I then asked the
editor of a magazine called *Ingenue* if I could write for her
and she said yes, though what I would actually do was only
related to writing in that it involved ink and paper and words.
I went around asking people who were regarded as accomplished what they were like when they were the age of the *Ingenue* reader. I could now say that it bored me beyond
measure, but that would not be true at all, for I had known
real boredom, I had survived being a child. I was not bored by
my subjects' answers because at that time I did not hear anything anyone else said, I only heard my own voice, I was only
interested in my own story.

The magazine called *Ingenue* was owned by the same man
who owned the *National Lampoon*, and the two magazines
were in the same building. I must have gone up and down in
the elevator many times without paying attention to anything
or anyone, for I cannot remember anything particularly, except this: one day a man, perfectly handsome and wonderful
(that was how he appeared to me on a first look), and kind
(that was how he appeared to me after many looks), ex-

changed some words with me, and at the end of it he said to me that he would like me to meet his friend George Trow. That man who spoke to me in the elevator, his name was Michael O'Donahue and he is dead now, but at the time that I met him, he was at the center of a group of men who earned their living by telling jokes and making people laugh. I perhaps should have thought that was strange, since less than ten years had passed since I left the island on which I was born and on which I had spent the first sixteen years of my life; I was then twenty-three. On the island where I grew up, jokes were told as a form of entertainment, but everyone had a joke, and jokes were so common and everyday that when something serious and important had to be done, someone would have to announce, in a serious and harsh way, that what was about to take place was not a joke.

Michael O'Donahue introduced me to George Trow and George befriended me. George then was a writer for a magazine called *The New Yorker*, a magazine that has since gone out of business, though there exists now a magazine by that name. George was the first person to listen to me, George was the first person I made laugh with an offhand observation, George was the first person to make me understand that what I said mattered, George was the first person to make me hear my unconscious voice before other people heard it so. George took me to events that featured the important people involved in the world of disco or humor or other things which were of interest to him and which he felt should be of interest to me.

I did not know anything then, I do not know anything now,

but I knew even less then. I read everything, I read without discrimination. One day I said the word "utilize" while describing something to George and he told me that I must never say "utilize" because the word "use" would do very well, and he went out and bought for me a copy of Fowler's *Dictionary of Modern English Usage* and I never said the word "utilize" again, and I always want to correct people when they say "utilize" but I never do, because they are not me and I am not George Trow.

I lived then in rooms in other people's apartments, or I lived in their apartments while they were away in Paris, or while they went off to live for a short time with people they had only just fallen in love with; I had no place of my own because I had no money. I was always avoiding the telephone calls of the people who were away in Paris, or the presence of the people who had let me live in one of the rooms in their apartment, or the presence and the telephone calls of the people who had allowed me to live in their apartments because they had gone off to live with the new person with whom they had fallen in love. Is it possible to live like that in New York now? I do not know. I had no money, I had no place to live, and I almost never could afford to buy myself my own food.

At the time I met Michael O'Donahue in the elevator, I had already come to make an object of myself. I had cut off my hair to a short boy-like length and I had bleached it from its natural black color to blond; I had shaved off my eyebrows completely and painted in lines with gold-color eye makeup where my eyebrows used to be. I could not afford to buy new clothes and so I bought old used-up ones and I wore them as if they were the only clothes an interesting person would wear. I had never liked nylon stockings and I could not comfortably wear high-heeled shoes, and so I wore white anklets and old saddle shoes and I wore them as if they were the only kinds of things to wear on your feet if you were an interesting person. I thought of myself as an interesting person, though I had no idea what that meant and I did not care if anyone else agreed with me. In fact, many people did not agree with me. People of every kind would stare at me, and mostly with hostility. That did not bother me at all. Young black men and women would stare at me and laugh at me and then say something insulting. That in particular did not bother me at all; in fact, I rather liked that, it was most familiar. I had grown up in a place where many people were young and black and men and women, and I had been stared at and laughed at, and insulting things had been said to me: I was too tall, I was too thin, I was very smart; my clothes had never fit properly there, I was flat-chested; my hair would not stay in place. And so when the young black men and women would stare at me and make fun of me, I was used to it, I did not feel threatened by it at all, it was familiar. And even now, especially now, I think they, young black men and black women, are the only people whose opinion I want to seek out, whose attention I want to provoke.

On that day I met Michael O'Donahue in the elevator and he asked me if I would like to meet his friend George Trow I was wearing jodhpurs made out of a beautiful beige, twilled cotton; a plain white cotton blouse; a deep brown fitted-at-the-waist jacket; a brown plastic brooch that looked like a man's wristwatch, but instead of hands and numbers my brooch had a dog's head drawn on its face; and around my neck I wore a bright yellow silk scarf that had printed on it some kind of small, not American, dog. I had a number of funny little hats in all sorts of colors and all sorts of materials. On the day I met Michael O'Donahue in the elevator, I wore a beige one that was in the shape of small round cake, and I wore it cocked on one side of my head, so that it looked capricious or just stylish, I did not care which. I walked then the way I walk now, I talked then the way I talk now. I never wear those clothes now, not even the scarf; they do not fit me anymore.

I had wanted to be a writer before I met George, I had wanted to be a writer before I met Mr. Shawn. I do not know if I would have become the writer that I am now if not for a set of events. George took me many places with him, sometimes just for my companionship, sometimes just to feed me. One night he took me to a restaurant that was on Twenty-eighth Street between Lexington and Park Avenue, and that restaurant served Lebanese food. I said something, I do not remember what, but it pleased George and he laughed in the biggest of his big laughs and he said that he would take me to meet Mr. Shawn and I did not know then who Mr. Shawn was but I agreed to it all the same.

It was a day in April, a cold day, and I wore not clothes for comfort, warmth, but clothes that I liked: I wore a pink-and-white silk dress, a dress that had been fashionable in the 1930s, and my brown jacket, the one I usually wore with jodhpurs. If I can't remember what Mr. Shawn looked like when I first met him that spring in 1974, it is only because he looked the same to me as when I saw him for the last time in November of 1992, and not long after that he died. At that lunch I was asked to place my order first, out of courtesy, of course, but I did not know that, and I ordered the most expensive meal on the menu, because either I was hungry right then or I did not know when I would have such a good meal again. I was quite ashamed that George ordered something that cost half as much as mine did and Mr. Shawn had only tea and a slice of cake, and when I saw what they had ordered I really thought it was because my own meal had cost so much that there wasn't enough money left for them to eat properly.

It was because George loved Mr. Shawn that he wanted me to meet Mr. Shawn and introduce Mr. Shawn to someone who might write for him and in that way give Mr. Shawn some amusement, some joy; I felt then, and still do now, that George loved me and wanted to bring me into that part of his world. I loved George then and know that I still do now. Mr. Shawn did not think that I would make a Talk reporter, but he told George that I should try. It was five months later that I wrote my first piece, but it was only after I wrote that piece, only after Mr. Shawn read it and gave it a form, a life, that I knew it was writing, my writing, and it was through that piece of writing and Mr. Shawn's acceptance of it that I came to know writing, the thing that I was doing, the thing I would do, that thing that I now do, writing; it was through that first experience with giving Mr. Shawn some thoughts of my own on paper that I came to be the person writing that I am now.

I was born in St. John's, Antigua, and I spent the first sixteen years of my life there. Shortly after I turned sixteen years of age, I was sent to America by my family to work and earn money to support them. I did not like any of it at all. I did not like being sent away, and then I did not like sending them the money I had earned. By the time I met George, I talked about my family all the time and in such an obsessive way that I must have seemed insane. George did not think so, Mr. Shawn did not think so. That first piece I wrote was about the carnival that immigrants from the English-speaking West Indies re-created in Brooklyn, New York. But to say wrote is misleading, for I did not think I was writing; I made some notes, observations of what I saw in the days before the actual carnival, and then I wrote down my impression of the carnival itself. The two things were separate, notes and observations, and I thought that when I gave them to Mr. Shawn he would have George rewrite the notes and make them sensible. Instead, notes and observations were printed, just as I had written them, and it is the just-as-I-had-written-them quality that makes me to this day suspicious of people, editors, giving me suggestions about how I should change one thing or another when I write.

As far as I knew then, I wanted to be a writer; as far as I knew then, I wanted to be that thing in particular, a writer, I did not want to be myself, I did not know what myself really was, I only did not want to be myself as I knew myself then, I wanted to be a writer. But I did not know how to do that, I did not know how writing was done. When at that moment Mr. Shawn published my words, my thoughts that I had on my mind, I knew I could be a writer, and I became a writer. The words I spoke, the thoughts in my head, that was my writing, and I did not need to have come from the people who had long straddled the world, I did not need to come from the people who had imagined and then made real the world in which I lived. That moment became my own. In the beginning was my word and my word became the world as I ordered it to be. If it now sounds too bold, if it now sounds too made up, if it now sounds too in retrospect, all the same it is true: when I saw my words and my own thoughts, as I had put them down on paper in the pages of a magazine authorized (and that is the real word for it, "authorized") by Mr. Shawn, I became a writer and that writer became me. That is the person who is writing this.

Until I wrote about the West Indian Day carnival in Brooklyn, I had appeared in the Talk of the Town section of *The New Yorker* as a person who said interesting things. Not long after that, I began to write my own contributions to the Talk of the Town. I wrote in the "We" voice and I did not like it a little bit at first and then I did not like it altogether. And that was the point, and that was the good thing: it was not meant for me to settle in to writing "We" and I only see that now. It was only afterward, long afterward, that I came to see that writing for the Talk of the Town was a kind of apprenticeship, that I was supposed to do it for just so long and then go on to my actual writing.

The anonymity of Talk then was a gift, and I only see that after Talk stories began to be signed. I feel sorry for those writers who now have to sign their names to Talk pieces. How young I was then and how old I felt then. I had just started to write and almost immediately I felt I wanted to write important things. And so at the beginning of each year I would make my New Year's wish be: May this be the year I write fiction. And the year would wear on and I did not write fiction; instead, I wrote for Talk and, feeling confined by it I began to write my Talk stories as little stories in themselves, as little experiments. I wrote a Talk story in the style of the Nancy Drew books, I wrote a Talk story in the form of an expense account, I wrote about growing up in Antigua. One day I wrote my first short story; it was about growing up in Antigua and it was one sentence long and it went on for three typewritten pages. One day I wrote an entire novel about growing up in Antigua.

What did I love most then? I loved my friends and I loved being at *The New Yorker*. My friends were all at *The New Yorker*. I loved Mr. Shawn, and he was the editor of *The New Yorker* and the person for whom I wrote then and who is now dead, but when I write even now, I think of him, perhaps especially even now, perhaps more than ever even now. He did not like everything I wrote, and when he didn't he never told me, we never discussed it. Sandy Frazier and I had a joke about what happened to our writing that Mr. Shawn did not like and did not ever bring up again. It was this: Lord Mountbatten, an Englishman, had been killed by the IRA, when they blew up his yacht on which he had been a passenger while sailing off the coast of Ireland. Sandy and I for very different reasons hate aristocrats of every kind, but especially English ones, and we were perhaps the only two people in the world then who actually felt sympathetic to the IRA when they blew up Lord Mountbatten's yacht. When Mr. Shawn never mentioned our Talk stories that had been submitted, which meant that they would never be printed, we began to refer to our stories as taking trips with Lord Mountbatten on his last fateful sail off the coast of Northern Ireland. A Talk story I wrote about a mouse running over me in the middle of the night met such a fate. The mouse ran over me because I was sleeping on the floor. I had no money to buy a proper bed and so I slept on the floor, first on newspapers and then later on an old mattress I found on the street. I am so afraid of rodents that I am sure I was one in a former life. I wrote of my fear and I wrote of my poverty. That story was never printed. I do not regret it, I do not miss it.

I miss Mr. Shawn, I miss the friends I had then, I do not miss my youth. I miss Mr. Shawn because for a writer, no matter your age, to know such a voracious reader, a reader who liked to read what you had written, just what I had written, was a gift so rare, and I have never been given it again, I do not know why. And when I say that I do not miss my youth and yet that I miss my friends, what do I mean, for Sandy Frazier is my best friend and I talk to him almost every day that there is a day. What do I mean, what do I mean? Only that George Trow will not go to Mr. Shawn and insist that the wall separating his office from Tony Hiss's be removed, so that they can write Talk stories with their typewriters facing each other, and then one day go to Mr. Shawn and insist that the wall be put in its place again because Tony wore a tie that annoyed him. Or this: Sandy Frazier standing on his desk before a window that looked into Kennedy Fraser's office, and while she was sitting at her desk, which was in front of a window that looked into Sandy's office, he started to take off his clothes, and all along she pretended not to notice, but then when he got to his underpants, she suddenly got out of her chair and pulled down her window shade. I miss all those people I knew then; I see them now, but it is not the same, and it cannot be the same: Mr. Shawn is dead, I am now over fifty years of age, I live far away from New York City.

And yet and yet: Mr. Shawn will never be dead for me, and my youth, and all the friends and events that came with them, can never be dead. For when I sit down to write anything, anything, I cannot help but think about George Trow with the thick bunch of yellow hair growing out of his head, and he introduced me to Sandy (Ian) Frazier, and the world after that was muddled, and the world after that was so clear, is so clear; all things, everything not seen through this lens, is a mistake, a very big mistake!

West Indian Weekend

Speeding by Taxi Across the Manhattan Bridge with Sassy Antiguan Jamaica Kincaid—Toward Dimanche Gras, on the Grounds of the Brooklyn Museum, on the Third Day of the Seventh Annual West Indian–American Day Carnival:

"There are several things you ought to know," said Jamaica. "First of all, you are going to see The Mighty Sparrow, who is the No. 7 calypso singer. Secondly, you are going to see 'Ole Mas.' The 'Ole Mas' is a spoof. This year, there is going to be an important 'Ole Mas' about New York Transit Authority buses. There will be men dressed as women—my friend Mr. Errol Payne told me all about it. One man will have a big over-stuffed bust. He'll have a sign saying 'I Own de Bus.' Another man will have a big overstuffed bust trailing behind him. *He'll* have a sign saying 'I Lose de Bus.' But what I really have to do is to tell you about 'jumping up.' 'Jumping up' is a very important West Indian concept. You 'jump up' when things get to be so exciting you just can't sit still, and that happens all the time during Carnival. I love to go to Carnival now, because when I was growing up my mother *would not let me 'jump up.'* My mother was *so strict.* All I wanted was to 'jump up' at Carnival and get little patent-leather shoes from America. My mother would never let me 'jump up,' and she would never let me have shoes from America, because she said they would fall apart in the first rain. Anyway, when I was fourteen we had a real row because I wanted to march with a band at Carnival. I was going to be in a band dressed up as bees and I would have been a worker bee. It wasn't much, but my mother just wouldn't let me do it. So we compromised, and she got me a pair of plaid sneakers from America. She was right, of course. As soon as they hit water, they fell apart."

At Dimanche Gras (Threatened by Rain), on the Grounds of the Brooklyn Museum:

There were a lot of seats set up around a big stage in the open air. On the back of each seat was a plastic bag that read "Fred Richmond for Congress," which would become useful if it rained. Jamaica introduced us to several dignified men who wore ribboned badges reading "Carnival Improvement Committee." Then she introduced us to La Belle Christine, the limbo dancer. "I'm the famous limbo-dance artist," said Miss Christine. "I performed on Friday night. I'm adjunct-professor of Ethnic Dance at City University. I'm America's No. 1

limbo-dance artist. I design my own costumes and I do my own choreography. I've got my B.A. I'm working on my M.A. I'm in *Who's Who Among Students in American Universities and Colleges: 1972–73.*"

We asked Miss Christine where she came from in the Caribbean.

"I'm from Montserrat," she said. " 'The Emerald Isle of Natural Beauty.' "

Then The Mighty Shadow—a young calypso singer who won the 1974 Road March in Trinidad and Tobago—came on-stage. He was dressed in beige pants, a navy-blue jacket, and an orange-and-white large-brimmed hat. He sang in a rapid-fire style to music that was staccato beyond syncopation. Jamaica said he was very slick. Then Alwyn Roberts—Lord Kitchener—came on. Lord Kitchener is a famous Calypso singer who has been popular for many years. He wore white pants, a black-white-and-yellow shirt, and a maroon cap. His music had a less rapid, less staccato beat. "I like Lord Kitchener very much," Jamaica said. "You see how less slick he is? Shirt, pants, and cap. None of that jacket stuff. When I was little, it was Lord Kitchener, The Mighty Sparrow, and Lord Melody. They were the ones. Lord Kitchener and Lord Melody did songs about loose women. The Mighty Sparrow was always slipping in a little social consciousness. Remember Patrice Lumumba? The Mighty Sparrow did a song about Patrice Lumumba. Lord Melody was the raunchiest. Lord Melody did a lot of songs they wouldn't play on the radio."

The audience was very well behaved. In the audience

there were people of every age—all enjoying the same thing and all well behaved. There were many men in coat and tie, and no one was sloppy. The white people in the audience weren't sloppy, but they were less well put together. Many of the white people there looked as if they were doing fieldwork for an extension course in Inter-Cultural Interaction: The Folk Experience. After Lord Kitchener performed, a man whose name we didn't catch sang a song about Trinidad called "God Bless Our Nation." The chorus went:

> It's fantastic, yes it is, the way
> how we live as one.
> In integration, our nation is
> second to none.
> Yes, the Negroes, the white man,
> the Chinese, the children play
> together in the sun,
> In this wonderland of calypso, in
> this wonderland of steel bands.

Then The Mighty Sparrow came on. He wore blue polyester pants and a multicolored shirt, and had a whistle around his neck. He sang a song called "Come See Miss Mary," which was—well, *suggestive*, and then he sang a song called "We Passed That Stage." He sang:

> Project an image of honesty and
> courage.

Put decency on front page.
Show wisdom not rage.
You must remember we passed
that stage.

Later (During the Rain) at Dimanche Gras:

After The Mighty Sparrow went off, a light rain began to fall. A steel band began to play, and people "jumped up"—all over but especially on the stage. Many people made use of their "Fred Richmond for Congress" plastic bags to keep the rain off their heads. One person who did this was Marcia Manners, the 1974 Carnival Queen. The band was good, and people had a fine time. It was very pleasant to "jump up" in the light rain. We had a good time talking with Ruddie King, who said he introduced steel bands in this country, and who told us how West Indian–American Day parades used to be in the old days when they were held in Harlem—starting at 110th Street and going up to 150th, ending with a celebration at the Rockland Palace. He showed us a group of props he had assembled for an "Ole Mas." There was a big clock, there was a figure of a man in a white pith helmet, there was an old pushcart, and there was an old-fashioned coal scuttle. Mr. King said that this "Ole Mas" was called "Behind Time." Then the rain got heavier. We took refuge in a booth where Mrs. Lezama, wife of Carlos Lezama, the hardworking man who organizes the Carnival each year, was presiding over pots of souse, *rôti*, and other West Indian food. We had some souse and some ginger beer made with fresh ginger, and then the rain really came down, spoiling the "Ole Mas." At five minutes past midnight, there was a cloudburst. Most people left. A dozen people went by under a tablecloth, still dancing. We left soon afterward. We found out the next day that Mr. Lezama and his co-worker Mr. Herman Hall stayed until the rain stopped, late in the morning, to properly look after the chairs, the stage, and other rented equipment.

Report from Jamaica on the History of Carnival:

"Errol Payne is an impressive-looking man who is the vice-president of art and culture of the West Indian–American Day Carnival Association. He is considered Trinidad and Tobago's Carnival ambassador to North America, and this is why: he has been entering costumes in band competitions since 1946; in 1956, he was made a Grand Knight of the Carnival Court for life; one of his winning costumes, 'Peacock,' was once used as a postage stamp for Trinidad and Tobago; he has had so many winning costumes that for a few years he was asked not to compete in costume contests in Trinidad and Tobago; his authority on costume-making is so widely respected that other costume-makers often come to him for assistance. So, naturally, if you want to know anything about Carnival, you ask him. This is what he says: 'Carnival started in Trinidad in the days of slavery, when the slave masters were

French. Around Christmastime, the slave masters would celebrate with eating and drinking and dress themselves up in costume. The slaves would be allowed to celebrate, too, and it was the only time they could dress themselves up and pretend they were anything they wanted. A man could pretend he was a king or a prince. They didn't have fine things to dress up in, so they would use old rags and old things to do it. That was the beginning of "Ole Mas." After slavery was abolished, the ex-slaves went into the streets, singing and dancing and beating drums, and that was Carnival. It was also with the slaves that calypso music was born. If a slave master was standing in the presence of two or three slaves and they wanted to say something that they didn't want him to know about, they would start singing it in picong tone, which is broken English, and patois French. That was their way of communicating with each other without the slave master's knowing what they were saying. Ever since then, Carnival has been growing like a wild vine, and nobody can stop it!' "

Excerpt from program of West Indian–American Day Parade down Eastern Parkway to Prospect Park:

> While it is true that Carnival is a very informal
> affair you are kindly urged to refrain from danc
> ing inside of costume bands on Eastern Park
> way. You may dance in front of them or behind
> because it is not right for bandleaders to spend

months of sleepless nights, a lot of money and
to work under all poor type of conditions and
then the public get inside of bands on Carnival
Day; Thus not allowing the bands to display
their pretty costumes.

Jamaica Reports on the West Indian–American Day Parade:

"I got to watch the parade from the second-best platform of
dignitaries. The first-best platform of dignitaries was reserved
for politicians. West Indians are the only group of people I
know who still have a great deal of respect for politicians,
men of the cloth, and schoolteachers, and anyone who makes
a career in any of the above fields automatically becomes dignified. I saw Shirley Chisholm. She sat with her legs crossed
at the ankles. Howard Samuels was there. No one seemed to
recognize him, and he looked like a man who had got himself
invited to the wrong party. Soon after, the first float appeared.
It carried the Carnival Queen and her lady-in-waiting. The
Queen looked regal enough in her long white gown and silver
crown, but, instead of waving to the crowd and smiling like a
dummy (the way queens usually behave), she was snapping
her fingers, wiggling her hips, and shuffling her feet, all at the
same time. I liked her very much and personally think she's
going to start a new vogue in royal public behavior. Then
came the bands. Now, here, when you say bands you don't
mean people playing musical instruments together in har-

mony but people wearing costumes in harmony. That is, they
pick a theme, and each member of the band wears a costume
that supports it. The bands had names like Caribbean Fragrance, Fiesta South of the Border, Vision of Beauty, The
Dream of Attila, Sailors Ashore in France, Splendor in Siena,
and Dreaming Through the Ages. Quite a few of these fan-
tasies took the shape of giant insects and birds, some were
fishes, and some were dragons, and some I just couldn't figure
out. They were quite wild and extravagant. The colors most
often used were red, orange, and yellow. Everything was
trimmed with gold and silver braiding. Some costumes had
such elaborate skirts that little wheels had to be attached for
mobility. Soon after this wave of fabulously alarming creatures
passed by, things at the dignitaries' platforms got as boring as
things at dignitaries' platforms can get. The remaining bands
were ten blocks away, 'jumping up' for their own pleasure, and
were in no great hurry to entertain dignitaries. Mrs. Chisholm
kept waving; poor Mr. Samuels looked even more lost than
before. I felt hungry and went to get something to eat. I
bought a rice-and-peas-and-chicken-and-pork dish from a
Panamanian woman, who said that she had made it herself. It
was so good I had two portions. Then I had a patty—West Indian pastry stuffed with ground meat—which I bought from
Tower Isle. I was told by the woman who sold it to me that
you can find Tower Isle patties in the frozen-foods department of your local supermarket. Of course, I liked that idea
very much, because you know an ethnic group has made it in
this country when you find its food at your local grocer. As

Lord Kitchener said to me, 'accessibility is the key to success.' After that, I had a large hunk of Shabazz Bean Pie. I say, without reservation, this is the No. 1 Third World dessert. In fact, every time I have some of it I think kindly of Mr. Shabazz and everybody with an 'X' after his name."

—*September 30, 1974*

Daytime Dancing, A Report

Every Friday, from noon to three o'clock, the young, upward-mobile, fun-loving, always-on-the-go set lunch and dance at La Martinique, a black discothèque at 57 West Fifty-seventh Street. Now, there are a few cultural traits that black people may want to deny (why, I'll never quite know), but there are some that they just can't escape. For instance, they can't deny that they know how to make dancing music better than anyone else, that they give better parties than anyone else, that they are better at dancing spontaneously than anyone else. The spirit of these three things makes a successful discothèque, and black discothèques are better than anyone else's. I visited La Martinique a couple of Fridays ago, and here are some of the things I noticed about the place.

La Martinique is a very welcoming discothèque. It has real-wood chairs at small fake-marble-topped tables, soft lighting, a large dance floor that always seems freshly sanded, a bar where you will get good Screwdrivers (and it would be wise not to have anything but), and a cigarette machine that charges seventy-five cents for a pack of cigarettes and takes only quarters.

In the evenings, La Martinique becomes a regular discothèque, and the people who are responsible for the evening entertainment are not the same people who put on the lunchtime dancing affair. The people responsible for the lunchtime dancing are Pjay Jackson, a secretary with an advertising agency; Roni Bovette; and Marvin Gathers. Pjay and the two men have a corporation that they call The Open Nose Production. It's a funny name but not unusual. It seems that whenever two or more black people go into the disco-party business in New York they give themselves names like A Nautilus Production or A Critical Path Production or The Winston Collection. Usually, at a disco party given by any one of the groups mentioned above, you are expressly forbidden to wear blue jeans, sneakers, or any other kind of clothing that will make you look poverty-stricken.

Here are some of the things I noticed about the people at La Martinique:

The people who go dancing there at lunch offer a special look at a new class of black people. It's the class whose men are particularly fond of well-tailored suits made up in a polyester fabric, wear moderately high-heeled shoes, have their hair styled in a small, neat Afro, smoke Kool or Pall Mall cigarettes, and never say to a young lady, "Hey, sugah, what you doin'?" Clarence McDade, a sales representative for DHJ Industries, at 1345 Sixth Avenue, is a good example of this. He was wearing a maroon suit that was sedate in cut and fit. He said about dancing at lunchtime at La Martinique, "I come here on Fridays because it's a way of letting off tensions. The setup is nice, the crowd is nice, most of the men are junior executives, like myself. When I go dancing in the evening, I usually patronize places like Leviticus, Gatsby's, and Nemo's, but every Friday I come here."

The women look something like this: pants suits or stylishly cut dresses made from another kind of polyester fabric, six-inch wedge platform shoes, plastic jewelry, and hair styles that suggest the use of a great deal of Dixie Peach Bergamot, a perfumed hairdressing pomade. This genre of black-female grooming has two things going for it: it is constantly pushed in the magazine *Essence*, and it is often marketed under the heading "Easy Elegance."

Dancing at lunchtime at La Martinique is reasonably priced. Not only will two-fifty allow you to dance but it will also entitle you to a lunch of cold cuts, salad, and fruit. The music isn't the top of black pop that you hear in most white discothèques. All the time I was there, I didn't hear my favorite song, "Kung Fu Fighting." The music that Ray, the resident d.j., is most fond of is long album cuts by B. T. Express, L.T.D., MFSB, Brian Auger, Manu Dibango, Hot Chocolate, The Bar-Kays, and the Average White Band.

There is one advantage to going dancing in the daytime, and Jimmy Jackson, who works at a post office somewhere in Brooklyn, pointed it out to me just before I left. "I work during the nights, so it's hard for me to get out," he said. "This is just the right thing for me."

Actually, it's just the right thing for everybody. This is not the first time I've danced in the middle of the day on Friday. When I was a little girl, in something like the equivalent of kindergarten, in the Caribbean, every Friday we got a longer recess period than on the other days of the week. Then some of us would gather at one end of the schoolyard, grab each other around the waist, and start dancing up and down while we chanted, "Tee la la la, congo. Tee la la la, congo." We didn't know what it meant, but we would chant it over and over again until the end of the recess. I liked Fridays just for that. It was the one time I was free to be sweaty and have fun. I also liked it because, according to my teacher, Mrs. Tanner, a very fat lady, whom we called Muddy Bottom Tanner behind her back, our behavior was becoming only to savages. How I did want to be a little savage! I bet they never had to take cod-liver oil every day, or eat porridge in the mornings, or wear cotton anklets when all the other girls were wearing nylon anklets. And, after not having to do any of that, they probably got to "Tee la la la" every day for as long as they liked. Mrs. Tanner would not understand or approve of lunchtime dancing at La Martinique.

—*January 6, 1975*

The Magic Is Blue

❦

Recently, we saw Blue Magic, the black five-man vocal group from Philadelphia, perform at the Felt Forum, and they were so incredibly good that they revived for us the word "copacetic." Not many things ever get to be copacetic these days. A truly outstanding thing might be called "cool" or "right on" or "solid" or "together," but very rarely is it outstanding enough to be called copacetic. Blue Magic, though, is outstanding enough to be called that. Blue Magic is the promise of The Temptations (who could be called "cool" or "right on" or "solid" or "together") fulfilled.

Blue Magic performing: Five peanut-brown men onstage, wearing identical sky-blue, formally tailored suits, white shoes, white bowlers, and singing, in the sweetest harmony possible, love songs. The lead singer has a choirboy tenor voice, and one of his tricks is to hold a note until he gets at least three standing ovations. A couple of times at the Felt Forum, he got five. But the real thrill in seeing Blue Magic is the way they dance. Every set of movements seems to culminate in pirouettes. Sometimes they pirouette while standing up straight, sometimes while leaning backward, sometimes while leaning forward, sometimes with hands on hips, sometimes with arms outstretched, sometimes while appearing to curtsey. It is at once graceful and dazzling. At the end of the performance, they disappear in a big cloud of blue smoke. Just like that.

A few days after seeing them at the Felt Forum, we saw them in the bar at the Dorset Hotel, on West Fifty-fourth Street, and they were having refreshments. They introduced themselves: Ted Mills (the lead singer), Vernon Sawyer, or Y.M.P., short for Young Mr. Plush (the group's clothes designer). Wendell Sawyer (Vernon's brother and the group's vocal arranger), Keith Beaton (the group's choreographer), and Richard Pratt. They were all wearing neatly tailored suits made of natural-looking fibre, and they all wore tons of expensive-looking jewelry around their necks and on their fingers.

We asked them how old they were, and Ted said that none of them was younger than twenty-three or older than twenty-six.

We asked Keith how he went about his choreography, and he said, "Well, I figure it out mathematically, and we all have good memories. Like one song might have fifty to seventy-five different steps, and we will have to do twenty-five of them before Ted sings the first note. Sometimes, while Richard and Vernon are doing one thing, me and Wendell will be doing the opposite. I have my own ideas, plus I borrow from the old

Temptations. I have even borrowed things from female artists. See, most groups just dance and do steps with no conception of what's going on, but we try to tell the story. The way I figure it, the way we move isn't ordinary, it's out of this world. It's kind of magic, really."

After that, Ted Mills told us that though Blue Magic was part of the W.M.O.T. Productions Family in Philadelphia, the group itself is a corporation known as Mystic Dragon. We asked him what W.M.O.T. stands for, and why a corporation is called Mystic Dragon. He said, "W.M.O.T. stands for We Men Of Talent, and they are responsible for our record production. Mystic Dragon means that we own ourselves. It means that Vernon will not just design clothes for Blue Magic or Keith choreograph only for Blue Magic, and Wendell can arrange voices for other people as well. Richard is our accountant, and I can handle corporate business. We are very smart. I was studying law when I first joined the group, and we each read at least one book every four days. We chose the name Mystic Dragon because it reflects Blue Magic. We are in tune with the harmony of man itself. We are what happens when the limited seeks the unlimited. One day, through us, I hope to reveal the secrets of Blue Magic."

Just before we left, we told them that Blue Magic's performance was so appealing it made us wish we had lots of miniature sets of Blue Magic to carry with us wherever we go. They laughed, and Vernon Sawyer said, "That's such a nice idea we just might start working on it."

—*August 11, 1975*

A Commercial Party

❧✦❧

The other evening, Revlon, the big cosmetics company, threw a party in the first-floor-accessories department (hats, gloves, scarves, cosmetics, things like that) of Bloomingdale's, to celebrate the opening of the movie *Mahogany*, starring Diana Ross, and to introduce a new line of "Orient-inspired" colors, called China Bronze, in their Touch & Glow makeup. Since Miss Ross is the model for Touch & Glow in the movie, we naturally assumed that China Bronze was another line of colors for black women. Great. Black is beautiful, true, but it never hurts to try to be more beautiful. Well, we were wrong.

At the party, we walked in and immediately had our picture taken by a couple of photographers from Polaroid, who then pasted the photograph on a black piece of cardboard and told us that this framed picture of us was taken by the SX-70 camera. We checked out a rumor that Diana Ross might make an appearance and were told that she was in California, about to have a baby. We looked around and saw Tony

Perkins, who also stars in the movie, wearing a denim shirt and denim pants; Ben Vereen, wearing a handsome black velvet suit, which he told us was designed specially for him by Jacques Bellini; Jacques Bellini, wearing a handsome black velvet jacket, which he told us he had designed for himself; some unrecognizable well-dressed, smiling people eating Chinese-style spareribs and fried chicken; lots of other unrecognizable well-dressed, smiling people drinking champagne; and more unrecognizable well-dressed, smiling people watching scenes from *Mahogany*, on a color television set. What we didn't see were any black women who looked as if they might be wearing the new China Bronze colors.

Just as we were about to inquire what, exactly, was going on, a slim, pretty, non-black young woman, wearing a cluster of yellow flowers in her hair, a brightly colored shirt, and black pants, came up to us and said that her name was Kathy Fields, that she was a makeup consultant for Revlon, that she was with the China Bronze "collection," and that she was actually wearing one of the new hues. We took a good look at her face. It was cherry red, as if she had just stuck it in a hot oven. "I think it's a dynamite look," she said.

"But aren't these colors for black women?" we asked.

"Well, yes," she said. "But—"

Before she could finish, a very light-complexioned Negro man who was standing nearby jumped in and said, "No, they aren't."

The man introduced himself as Ron Marablé, beauty consultant for Revlon. Then he told us, "They're not black cosmetics. People are no longer into that. There is no longer such a thing as black cosmetics. We don't believe there is a different makeup for different people. There are many different skin tones in the world, and black is just one of them. I know. I went to art school for eight years, and then I went to Europe. I did Sophia Loren in Rome. I studied with her makeup artist for a year. I have done Melba Moore, Freda Payne, Nina Simone, Virna Lisi, Nancy Wilson, and—oh, Coretta King. Don't forget that. She was my favorite—Coretta King. I used to be the beauty editor for *Ebony*. I used to do before-and-after—I would take a woman and make her over. I would take an ugly woman and make her pretty. But this is a makeup for any woman. Any woman can wear it. We have a range of colors here. Bronze, copper, rust—all the warm earth colors. They're going over well. On the first day, we sold three thousand dollars. Today, we did twenty-five hundred. And tomorrow we hope to do over three thousand."

—*October 27, 1975*

Time with Pryor

Two things we know about Richard Pryor for sure: he is the funniest man in America, and, after Muhammad Ali, he is the baddest person anywhere. "Bad" here does not mean rotten or no good. It means being so extraordinarily good at doing something that for someone to call you the greatest, or anything like that, does not quite measure up to describing how incredible you are. Only the word "bad" will do. For instance, not long ago we saw Pryor performing at the Felt Forum, in Madison Square Garden, and he said things that are usually considered uncomplimentary about blacks, whites, and women, and the audience, which was made up of blacks, whites, and women, laughed and laughed.

He was in town the other day, and around dinnertime we stopped by his suite at the Regency Hotel for a chat with him. Before we had a chance to say hello, he stuck a finger out and showed us a ring he was wearing and said, "Look at this ring. It's nice. Ain't pimpy at all." We looked. It was a slim, plain gold band decorated with three delicately set diamonds. Then we looked at him. We had never before seen him close up, and noticed that he is quite handsome. He is tall, slim (he was dieting, he said), with a boyish face that is especially nice when he smiles. He was wearing tapered gray trousers, a mottled black-and-white sweater, and brown mules. In his rooms with him were a woman he introduced as his girl friend, his manager, his valet, and his jeweller.

We spent three hours with him, and during that time this is what happened: he bought a gold necklace with a heart-shaped, diamond-studded pendant for the woman he had introduced as his girl friend; he bought a gold ring for his manager and a gold ring for his valet; he wrote a check for sixteen hundred dollars to his jeweller; he ordered a dinner of sweet-and-sour fish from Greener Pastures, a health-food restaurant not far from the hotel; he picked up his spinach with his bare hands and said with a British accent, "I like my spinach squeeze-dried, don't you?"; when the telephone rang, he spoke into his mules; during dinner, he watched *The CBS Evening News with Walter Cronkite* and mimicked Walter Cronkite many times; after dinner, he disappeared for a while with a copy of *U.S. News & World Report*. When he was not mimicking Walter Cronkite, these are some of the things he said: "I am now a vegetarian. I was standing at the corner of Forty-second Street, and this man came up to me and said, 'Rise, and go forth and be a vegetarian.' One thing I can say— I was lucky he didn't pick my pocket. Vegetables are funny. They have a great sense of humor. You drop their seeds in the ground and they rub around in the dirt and then they grow up and you can eat them. Politicians are always doing things to Negroes. One will be standing on his head, another on his ass, and another on his foot. Politician to Negro: 'Look, buddy, this is what I can do for you.' Negro to politician: 'Man, will you take your foot off my mother?' I'm trying to figure out things to sell to the Chinese. They don't dig Joe DiMaggio. How about an album of Mao's greatest hits? I was born under the sign of funny. I haven't met the other people born under that sign yet, but I think a couple of them became scientists. You know how I get to be funny? I go to sleep for about a year. I wake up with cobwebs all over my face. I roll them up in a large ball with milk and sugar, eat it quickly, and then I start laughing. People say, What's so funny? I tell them. They start laughing. Then I have lunch. Some of the things I say are true, some are not, but it all happened."

—*January 12, 1976*

Bells and Drells

✦

We recently got an early-morning phone call from our friend Weldon Arthur McDougal III. He is the energetic promo man for Philadelphia International Records, the Philadelphia-based, black-owned record company, and he reminded us that once in a conversation with him we had said that, along with Brenda and the Tabulations, Jay and the Techniques, and Martha and the Vandellas, Archie Bell and the Drells, the black singers from Houston, Texas, had the best name for a singing group, and that their two hit songs from the late sixties, "Tighten Up" and "I Can't Stop Dancing," had remained in the best-for-dancing category. "Well," McDougal said, "Archie Bell and the Drells are now with us. They have a new album, and I'm bringing them to town tomorrow to meet New York, and then I'm throwing a party for them at Leviticus."

At noon the next day, with McDougal, we hopped over to the Statler Hilton hotel, where Archie Bell and the Drells were staying, to get a daylong view of them. McDougal, who was dressed from head to foot in black, introduced us around—first to Archie Bell and then to Willie Parnell, James Wise, and Lee Bell (Archie's brother), who make up the Drells. When we were introduced to Archie Bell, he said "Hey, what's happening, ain't *nothing* to it" in one breath. Later, we learned that this is his favorite way of greeting people. We focussed on Archie Bell, because the Drells deferred to him, and because, while the Drells wore a collection of patchwork-denim and polyester outfits, Archie Bell was wearing a smart-looking leisure suit. It was beige, with deep-brown stripes running down the pants legs, and the jacket had darts and tucks that made it fit snugly. After telling us how glad he was to be in New York, he said, "I would like to mention that we have one of the finest tailors in the country. He's from Houston, Texas, and his name is Johnny Burton. He makes clothes for people like the Temptations and James Brown. He made this suit I am wearing, and he made the suits we are wearing on our album cover—the ones with the little bells all over them." Then Archie Bell said, "We have been waiting so long to come back. When I had those hit songs 'Tighten Up' and 'I Can't Stop Dancing,' I was in the Army, so I couldn't do any entertaining. When I got out, I was cold. James and Willie and me have been working since we were in high school. We lived in the same neighborhood and went to the same high school. My brother Lee joined the group in 1969. But all the time we didn't have any hits we were working. We've been on the road for three hundred and twenty days out of a year. Sometimes three hundred and fifty.

We worked the South a lot. My mother always told us that we could do anything. She has seven children, all of them boys. You ever heard of Ricky Bell? He is a top college football player, and he is my brother."

At a quarter to one, McDougal, who had been busy all this time taking pictures, announced that it was time to make the first stop. The first stop was an autographing session at the record store Disc-O-Mat, which was a few blocks away from the hotel, and for the next nine hours this is what Archie Bell and the Drells did: At Disc-O-Mat, they autographed fifty records and about twice that number of publicity stills, and Archie Bell also autographed pictures of Ricky Bell. At a quarter past two, they went to Leviticus for rehearsal. At four o'clock, they left Leviticus and taxied up to the midtown offices of *Cash Box*, the music trade magazine, for an interview with a young reporter, who asked them questions like "Do your producers make you feel comfortable in the studio?" and "I'll confess that I'm a little ignorant about what you guys have been up to, so how about if we kind of clear this up?" On their way out, they met Steve Ostrow, the man who compiles the weekly album charts for *Cash Box*, and he told them that their new album had just débuted on the charts at No. 183. At five o'clock, the Drells took a taxi to their hotel, and Archie Bell went off to a Nunn Bush shoe store to buy a pair of shoes. At half past six, they were back at Leviticus for the party, wearing the same clothes they had been wearing earlier. There were lots of black people at Leviticus. There were even some easily recognizable black people there. We picked out

Lou Rawls, the singer; David Ruffin, the former lead singer of the Temptations; Don Covay, the important R. & B. singer from the sixties; and Harold Melvin, of Harold Melvin and the Bluenotes. At eight o'clock, Archie Bell and the Drells disappeared into the dressing rooms at Leviticus to change into their show clothes. At half past eight—show time—they reappeared, and they were quite incredible to see. They were wearing identical white skin-tight jumpsuits that had gold studs and brown bells running down the sides, and tight-fitting white bolero jackets over the jumpsuits, and white platform shoes. They sang most of the songs from their new album, plus "Tighten Up" and "I Can't Stop Dancing." The audience was very pleased, and cheered and danced. Archie Bell was very pleased. He said to us, "I could do this all day, all night."

—*February 9, 1976*

Lunchtime

❧❖❧

As the weather around here becomes more unbearable, little ways to divert yourself can become important. Nighttime is not a problem. You can take care of that by accepting every invitation that comes your way. Midday is another matter. What to do about lunch? So far, we have tried having it with different sets of people; we have tried having it with the same set of people; we have tried having it alone; we have tried not having it at all. Just the other day, we tried having our lunch while watching a Theatre at Noon production of Maria Irene Fornes' play *Dr. Kheal* at St. Peter's Church, which is on East Fifty-sixth Street, and this new way of having lunch was far better than anything else we had tried.

There are two shows put on every weekday—one at a quarter past twelve and the other at a quarter past one. We took the early show. We got to St. Peter's at noon sharp, taking our lunch along, as we had been given to understand we should do. At the door, we learned that there was no admission charge but that donations were invited. We made our donation, walked in with a sandwich (ham salad) and a soft drink (ginger beer), and hoped for a good time. We got a good time. First of all, the theatre is a dimly lighted room with about fifteen medium-sized round tables, a red tablecloth on each table, and four chairs to each table. When we got there, about ten couples were already seated and were unpacking or eating their lunches. It was very cozy and comfortable-looking. We thought we would wait until the show got under way before we had our lunch, and then we were sorry, because we laughed so much. The show began with a man reading this from a piece of paper: "It is with great pleasure that I welcome Dr. Kheal to Theatre at Noon today. With this visit, Dr. Kheal is completing a cross-country lecture tour, which has taken him to more than fifty universities and colleges. After this lecture Dr. Kheal will be returning to Harvard, where he will resume his position as Distinguished Professor of Philosophy and Mathematics. I am proud to introduce—Dr. Kheal." Dr. Kheal came onstage. Dr. Kheal, played by a talented young actor named Richard Hamburger, was wearing formal evening clothes and white shoes with red shoelaces. He looked quite comical. Then he started to act quite comical. He walked over to a blackboard that was already on the stage, drew a large square on it, and wrote in the square lecture topics like "On Poetry," "On Ambition," "On Energy," and "On Truth." All in all, Dr. Kheal—or Richard Hamburger—was a funny man. Also, he said very funny things. The thing he said that we liked best was on the subject of energy. He said, "How does one do a million small things? One at a time. How does one do a million big things? One at a time. How does one do one big thing? Never."

—*February 16, 1976*

Free-ee-ee

We have become interested in a young black woman singer named Deniece Williams. We have become interested in her because she sings in a soft, sexy voice. It is a voice we haven't heard from young black women singers since the early sixties, when young black women singers sang in groups. We first heard Deniece Williams on the car radio. She was singing a song called "Free." She sang, "But I just got to be me, free, free-ee-ee." She sang most of the song in a clear soprano. Then, when she got to the "free-ee-ee" part, she shifted her voice upward—way, way up. It seemed effortless, and completely cool.

We saw Deniece Williams the other day. She was in town performing in a concert at the Felt Forum, where she was billed third in a lineup of four acts. We visited her in her dressing room shortly before she went onstage. A few friends and aides were with her. She wore a tight-fitting aqua-blue *satin jump suit* and gray satin platform shoes. She told us that

she is from Gary, Indiana; that she has been living in Los Angeles for the last four years; that she has been singing since
she was five; that she started singing in church; that when she
was seventeen years old she had a job as a salesgirl in a record
store, would sing along with the records, and began to think
of singing professionally; that years ago she recorded two sin-
gles for a label called Toddlin' Town; that she sang backup for
Stevie Wonder for three years; and that she now writes all the
songs she sings.

As she told us these things, she mixed some hot water,
lemon juice, and honey in a cup. Then she went into the
bathroom and closed the door. From where we were, we
could hear her sing in her upper register, "God is truly amazing." She sang this over and over, sometimes stretching out
and emphasizing the word "amazing." Then she sang some la-
la-la-las in the upper register. When she came out of the
bathroom, she said "Yuk."

Half an hour before she was due onstage, her road manager told her that, because of scheduling confusion, she
would have to go on second and could do only a twenty-
minute set, instead of thirty-five, as she had expected.

"Only twenty minutes?" she asked.

"Only twenty minutes," he said. "What are you going to
drop?"

"I guess I'll drop 'Slip Away' and the encore," she said.

After he left, she said, "I only got twenty minutes. I don't
care. I'm not going to feel bad about it. Nothing is going to
make me feel bad tonight."

Her band—five young men and a young woman, who was the backup singer—came in, and she told them what songs they would be doing. She said, "We'll do 'It's Important to Me,' not stopping but straight into 'That's What Friends Are For,' and then I stop and talk a little, and then we do ' 'Cause You Love Me, Baby,' 'If You Don't Believe,' and 'Free,' and that's it." She asked all the people in the room except the members of the band to leave, so that she and the band could pray before they went onstage. The songs she sang onstage were not as familiar to us as "Free," but then she sang that, too, and it was even better than listening to it on the car radio.

—April 4, 1976

Junior Miss

❧❀❧

Every year, fifty high-school seniors, representing our fifty states, compete in a televised national Junior Miss contest, sponsored by Eastman Kodak, Kraft Foods, and Breck Shampoo. The winner, America's Junior Miss, receives a ten-thousand-dollar scholarship to the college of her choice. Two days before New York's Junior Miss, Dawn Fotopulos, of Queens, was scheduled to go to Mobile, Alabama, to compete in the Junior Miss finals, she came over to Manhattan, accompanied by her mother, Mrs. William Fotopulos, and had her picture taken by the *News*, had a long lunch at the St. Regis, and was interviewed on three radio talk shows. When we first saw Miss Fotopulos, who is just under eighteen, she was standing near a rack of clothes in a shop on East Fifty-third Street, obliging the *News* photographer with the many poses he wanted her to assume. She was wearing a green wool blazer, green-and-white patterned knit slacks, and a white blouse. She has blue eyes, ruddy cheeks, and long light-

brown hair that flips up around her shoulders. Except for a
trace of mascara, lip gloss, and blue eye shadow, she wore no
makeup, and except for a small pair of pearl earrings she wore
no jewelry. After taking the shots in the store, the photographer told Miss Fotopulos that he wanted some shots of her
walking down Fifth Avenue. On Fifth Avenue he stood her a
few yards in front of him and told her to walk toward him
now—first slowly, then fast, then slowly again. He sat her on
one of the large planters that line the Avenue, tilted her head
forward, and told her to stay in that position. He told her to
gaze into a shopwindow displaying an assortment of women's
shoes. He told her to gaze into another shopwindow, which
had an assortment of women's sports clothes. Altogether, the
photographer took thirty-six pictures of Miss Fotopulos, and
for every single one of them she smiled.

At lunch at the St. Regis, Miss Fotopulos had roast beef,
lyonnaise potatoes, salad with French dressing, a glass of
milk, and fruit cup. She said that she had never before been
in a place like the St. Regis, or had lyonnaise potatoes. She
said, "I feel it's a dream. I feel I'm Cinderella or something.
All this special treatment. Everybody has been treating me as
if I were something special. It's so much fun. When I entered
this contest, I had no idea all this would happen. I found out
about the contest in *Seventeen*, and I wrote away for the
forms. I thought I wouldn't win, because I didn't have a local
sponsor. I was a candidate at large. But this is not like a
beauty contest. You don't have to wear a bathing suit. It
mostly has to do with scholarship and poise and grace. I have

a ninety-five-point-six average. I want to study medicine, and the money that I have already won will help me to do that."

Mrs. Fotopulos showed us a picture of her daughter wearing a long white sleeveless gown and carrying a bouquet of roses as she walked down a runway at the New York State contest, held in Syracuse, in February. Mrs. Fotopulos said, "She's made us so proud of her. You know, she has received a letter of congratulations from our state senator, and Governor George Wallace has sent her a letter welcoming her to the State of Alabama."

At the radio talk show we sat in on, the hostess told her the theme of the day: "Whether Our Idea of Mr. Right Has Changed or Not." She asked Miss Fotopulos questions like "Do you cook?" (Miss Fotopulos said yes), "Do you believe in Mr. Right?" (Miss Fotopulos said she thought that that might be a possibility), "Do you know who Bess Myerson is?" (Miss Fotopulos identified her as Miss America of 1945), "Do you have a pair of white gloves?" ("Well, I have to, because of the pageant"), and "Have you ever been to a prom?" (Miss Fotopulos said she hadn't).

Then the hostess asked Miss Fotopulos, "How do you feel about kissing?"

When Miss Fotopulos didn't reply immediately, the hostess said, "You're representing New York State and you don't have a stand on kissing?"

"Well, that's kind of unfair," Miss Fotopulos said. "I would never ask *you* how *you* feel about kissing."

—*May 10, 1976*

A Civic Gathering

⌘

THE TRAM: Last week, at an official midmorning ceremony, New York City opened to the public the Roosevelt Island Aerial Tramway, and thereby became the only urban community in the country with aerial-tramway transportation. The tramway, which serves the newly developed residential community on Roosevelt Island, runs thirty-one hundred and thirty-four feet alongside the Queensboro Bridge. There are two cars, and they are never in either station at the same time. The tramway has a maximum travelling speed of sixteen and three-tenths miles per hour, and each tramcar can carry a maximum of one hundred and twenty-five passengers, plus one operator. It takes three and one-half minutes to get from station to station.

When we arrived at the ceremony, which was being held at the Manhattan end of the run, we were met by a band called Al Madison and the Dixie Dance Kings, who played "When the Saints Go Marchin' In" over and over. On the boarding platform, there was some confusion. We saw a group of television reporters huddled together in a circle, all trying to talk at the same time. We later realized that they were interviewing Mayor Beame. We saw people boarding the tramway and then being asked by the conductor to debark. And we saw people drinking champagne. At ten forty-two the first tramcar, which carried dignitaries and members of the press, started across for Roosevelt Island. All the passengers, some with glasses in hand, cheered. It climbed up and up, reaching a peak of two hundred and fifty feet over the East River. Someone pointed out a fireboat gushing water and bellowing a greeting. The passengers cheered. Someone pointed out the United Nations. The passengers cheered. And when the other tramcar, coming from Roosevelt Island, passed by—empty—the passengers cheered for that, too. Then the eastbound car started to descend. It felt a little bit like a roller coaster, and the passengers, in unison, said "Whoooo!"

At Roosevelt Island, Mayor Beame, looking quite distinguished in a navy-blue suit, made a speech. He said, "We just took a ride over in this tramway, and, believe me, it's safe. This is the only aerial urban tramway in America, and it shows that New York is first, as always." Then he broke a bottle of champagne on the tramcar, and everybody cheered. Immediately afterward, there was a party for dignitaries, press, and Roosevelt Island residents in a park on Roosevelt Island. When we got to the party, Al Madison and his Dixie Dance Kings were playing away—only this time the tune was "Has Anybody Seen My Girl?" People were waiting in line for hot dogs, fried chicken, or a drink. They ate and drank two thousand hot dogs, thirty-five hundred pieces of chicken, eight hundred cups of Pepsi, eighteen hundred cans of Schlitz, one hundred and twenty bottles of New York State Gold Seal wine, and a case of champagne—all donated to the city.

—May 31, 1976

In Central Park

❧❧❧

LINES: The Hospitality Industry Foundation of New York City, which was recently set up by a group of New York restaurateurs, sponsored a Saturday food festival in the Mall and Literary Walk area of Central Park, and never before have we seen so many New Yorkers in one place having so much fun. Seventy-two restaurants participated, each with a booth and each selling one or two dishes, sometimes brought over from the restaurant and sometimes prepared on the spot. The visitors ate all the food sold by the participating restaurants, watched musicians and other performers perform, strolled around, and were polite to one another. The police estimated that more than three hundred thousand men, women, and children were present. There were so many people at the festival that a lot of them had to stand in lines, sometimes up to forty-five minutes, just to pay five dollars for a book of twenty tickets that enabled them to buy servings of food ordinarily sold as *spécialités de la maison* at the participating restaurants.

Then there were long lines for the food. The line at the "21" Club booth (steak tartare) was about two blocks long. The line at Marvin Gardens (mussels marinière and tabouleh salad) was about three blocks long. The line at Beefsteak Charlie's (slices of steak on a bun) was about four blocks long. There was a line at just about every food booth; and even to get a hot dog from a hot-dog vender who was not an official part of the food festival required waiting in line. No one seemed to mind.

We walked around, and here are some of the things we saw: a man juggling with cowbells and tambourines, a woman spinning a pie pan on a stick while doing somersaults, a man dressed in black doing magic tricks, a man dressed in black telling jokes about balloons, a clown, a mime, three flamenco dancers, a man playing an accordion, and a puppeteer. We met three boys collecting yogurt-cup tops at the Dannon Milk Products booth. They said that they had already collected seven thousand tops and that they hoped to have enough to be included in the *Guinness Book of World Records*. We stopped in at the Lost Children Area but didn't see any lost children. We saw six stout Spanish-speaking women with purple jumbo rollers in their hair relaxing under a tree. Near the end of the afternoon, we stopped by the bandshell, where various groups were performing. There was a rock group called Lance, and it was well received. There was a group called the West Side Singers, unaccompanied by any musical instrument. Its members looked like a Better Citizens Committee. They tuned up their voices by singing a few bars of "I'll Never

Fall in Love Again." Then they sang all the way through "Spinning Wheel," the old Blood, Sweat & Tears hit, with much vigor and in perfect harmony. By the end of it, they had lost a good many of the younger members of their audience.

—*June 7, 1976*

The Fourth

❧

Report from our friend Jamaica Kincaid:

I love America and Americans, because my father, who was an Antiguan, and who had worked as a civilian carpenter on the American base in Antigua during the Second World War, used to tell me how funny and great Abbott and Costello were, how funny and great the "Road" pictures with Bing Crosby and Bob Hope were, and how funny and great and attractive and smart Americans in general were. He would tell me all sorts of stories about Americans, who were always named Bud or Dick, and always the Americans were funnier, greater, smarter, and more attractive than anybody else, including him. At the end of every story about Americans, whom he always referred to as the Yanks, he would say, "Oh, the Yanks are a crazy bunch, but they have ideas, and you can't stop a man when he has ideas." But the thing my father said about Americans that made me love them the most was "The Yanks are great. Listen, if a Yank ever asks you if you can

do something and you can't do it, don't say 'No,' say 'I'll try.' "
My father was a snobby, critical, dignified man, who usually
said very little about anything. It was from him that I got the
full meaning of the term "It doesn't measure up." And I knew
that if he felt the way he did about Americans, you could
forget everything else. When I was nine years old, I added
an extra plea to my prayers. Up to then, I would say the
Twenty-third Psalm and the Lord's Prayer, and I would pray
that God would bless my mother and father and make them
live long enough to see me become a grown woman, and
would bless me and help me to be a good girl. But when I was
nine years old I started adding, "And please, God, let me go to
America." I did this for six years straight. As I grew older, I got
my own ideas about why I wanted to go to America. It had to
do with pink refrigerators; shoes that fall apart if you get
caught in the rain (because that way you can get a new and
different pair); the flip in Sandra Dee's blond hair as she
played a pregnant teen-ager in the movie A Summer Place;
Doris Troy, the way she looked and the way she sang "Just
One Look"; and, of course, Negroes, because any place that
Negroes are is cool.

On Sunday, I thought about all those things. I thought
about them because it was the Fourth of July and America
was two hundred years old and I found myself among millions
of Americans celebrating it by looking at a bunch of ships sail
up a river. It sounds silly, but that is one of the coolest things
I have ever done. I walked around and I saw some French
sailors mistakenly walk into an all-male bar on lower Tenth

Avenue looking for girls. I saw a group of black boys climb all the way to the very top of a steel arch on the abandoned West Side Highway to get a better view of things. They looked so neat—like a Cartier-Bresson photograph. And I met four natives of Poland who told me that after spending a week in New York they were sailing down the Mississippi to make a documentary on Mark Twain for Polish television. I felt tremendous, and for the first time in the eleven years I have lived here I felt like an American. I am very grateful to my father, who told me in his special way that, no matter what, I should always go with the cool people.

—*July 19, 1976*

Boz Scaggs

We went to the Wollman Memorial Rink, in Central Park, the other evening to hear Boz Scaggs, a singer who comes from Texas, perform. There are a few things we have always liked about Boz Scaggs. We like his performing name (Boz Scaggs) and we like his real name (William Royce Scaggs). We like the songs he sings, which are mostly his own compositions and are mostly about bad boys (as in a song called "Lowdown") and bad girls (as in a song called "Georgia"). When we saw him in the Park, we found other things to like. For instance, his live singing voice isn't at all far removed from his recorded singing voice; he talks with a nice Texas drawl; and he never once asked the audience if everybody was feeling all right or to accompany his singing with handclaps.

Boz Scaggs is not a new performer or a widely popular old performer. During the late sixties, he was a member of the Steve Miller Band, a San Francisco rock group. Since then, as a solo performer, he has had a "following." He's been very popular in cities like San Francisco, where he now lives, and New York. But his popularity seems to be getting national. We took a look at *Billboard*, the music-trade magazine, and saw that his latest album was in the Top Forty of both the regular chart and the black-music chart.

At the Wollman Memorial Rink, we saw many people wearing T-shirts that said simply "BOZ." Onstage, Boz Scaggs, a tallish, handsome man with brown hair that he wears swept back in a beatniklike style, wore blue pants, a red turtleneck sweater, and white sneakers. He was accompanied by some other musicians and by two pretty girl singers wearing white backless gowns. Sometimes he sang and played a white guitar, sometimes he sang and played a gold guitar, sometimes he sang and played a piano, and sometimes he sang and danced around. Almost always he said something about the song he was about to sing. He said, "This song is about a lady thing; it's about when it's all over," and he sang a song called "It's Over." He said, "This is a song about a cat who's inside doing time all because of a girl named Georgia. If you listen, you'll know why," and he sang "Georgia." Then he sang a song called "What Can I Say." It's our favorite Boz Scaggs song, because of these two lines: "Stop makin' like a little schoolgirl" and "Could be your lucky day, baby." That song made us very happy.

—August 30, 1976

A Gathering

PARTY: Among certain hip people in New York the word "party" has nothing to do with a dinner, or a birthday, or fishing, or hunting, or politics; rather, it has to do with going out to a discothèque, dancing for hours, and having a good time. They say to each other, "Let's party." Or—and this is the coolest way of saying it—"Let's party down." Songs have been written in which the word "party" alone, chanted against a funky beat, is the refrain. A man we know named Vince Aletti spends much of his time "partying," and, as can be imagined, he has a lot of fun. Vince Aletti loves to dance, knows just about all the good current dance songs, and writes a column on discothèque music for a national music-trade magazine. When popular-music critics write uncomplimentary articles about discothèque music, Vince Aletti, in turn, will write articles defending and promoting discothèque music. He has written articles defending the Trammps, Archie Bell and the Drells, and others. Last winter, in his column, he mentioned what a great song for dancing "Love to Love You Baby," by Donna Summer, was, and because he was the first person to write about that song and it became a big hit the record company gave Vince Aletti a gold record.

Every Saturday night, Vince Aletti goes dancing at a place in lower Manhattan called The Loft. On a recent Saturday night, he invited us to come along. On our way, he told us some things he thought we ought to know about The Loft. He said, "The Loft is open only on Saturday nights. It isn't like a regular discothèque; it's more like a private party. You just go and you meet your friends and you have a good time." (Vince Aletti is a very shy, retiring man in his late twenties, and it occurred to us that he would never go anyplace where his friends wouldn't be. Once, we introduced him to a man from the Midwest, and the man grabbed his arm and said, "Hey tiger, how ya doing? God love ya." It made him wince visibly.) Vince Aletti said that the people who go to The Loft to dance were called "guests"; that most of them started coming in at one o'clock; that to get into The Loft you had to show an invitation; that to receive an invitation you had to have a friend who was already a member submit your name; and that The Loft sometimes stayed open until seven o'clock in the morning.

We arrived at The Loft at a quarter past midnight, and for half an hour after that were the only customers there. Vince Aletti didn't have to show an invitation to get into The Loft. The doorkeeper knew him and greeted him this way: "Hi, Vince, what's happening?"

The Loft is not like any other discothèque we've ever been

to. It is made up of two floors. The downstairs is a recreation area. It has sofas and a bar, where fruit juices, fresh and dried fruits, peanut-butter-and-jelly sandwiches, and cookies are served without cost. Upstairs is where everyone dances. There are pretty, big balloons and paper streamers hanging from the ceiling. Above the dance floor, in a booth fashioned after an old Wurlitzer jukebox, is the disc jockey, whom we could see from below dashing around and arranging records. Vince Aletti told us his name was David Mancuso and that he was the proprietor of The Loft. Vince Aletti then led us up a narrow stairway to meet him.

Vince Aletti disappeared.

David Mancuso told us, "I have tried to make this place like a club I used to go to ten years ago called the Territorial Club, on 125th Street. I had just come to New York from Utica, and that club was just like what I thought a club in New York would be. It had a very warm and sincere atmosphere. The people were nice, the refreshments were nice. It was halfway between a bar and someone's house."

At half past twelve, David Mancuso played the first record of the evening. He said it was a song called "Sweet Sixteen" and that it was written by the Diga Rhythm Band, which is headed by someone who was and sometimes still is the Grateful Dead drummer. People started coming in. Vince Aletti reappeared and said, "I feel like I'm on a receiving line, because everybody who comes in here I know them, and I'm just greeting people." Then a song called "You Should Be Dancing" was played. Vince ran off to dance. Months ago, he told us that this was one of his favorite songs.

By two o'clock, the upstairs was filled with dancing people. Downstairs had many fewer people, and we went down to get a look at some of the guests. Quite a few people were wearing track or jogging outfits in bright colors. We saw one man dressed in what appeared to be the uniform of an officer of the Royal Navy, a couple dressed as Bedouin Arabs, and one man dressed in white ladies' platform shoes, white girls' knee socks, white jockey shorts, and white undershirt. We went back up to the dance area.

The record that was then being played wasn't by any group we recognized. It was just the sound of drums—about what you would expect to hear in a documentary film about primitive people. All the lights were off and people were dancing and making funny noises in the dark. The lights went on and everybody cheered. Then they went off again and everybody laughed. Then the music changed to a song by a group called Double Exposure. We saw Vince Aletti, and he was dancing vigorously to Double Exposure's song. He also danced vigorously to a song by a singer named D. C. LaRue and a song by the Emotions. He was less enthusiastic about a song by the Spinners called "Rubber-band Man." He said, "I like it when the Spinners get into it, 'cause it's kind of cute, but then it gets too cute." Then the disc jockey played a song by a group called Dr. Buzzard's Original Savannah Band. It is now Vince Aletti's favorite song, and when he danced he got so excited that he clenched both fists and thrust them into the air.

—*September 27, 1976*

Notes and Comment

A friend of ours, a young woman from Antigua, was here in the States for a short visit, and since we hadn't been to Antigua in more than ten years we asked her what things were like there.

"It's just like up here," she said. "We have everything down there that you have up here. Same fashions, same music. Except for Colonel Sanders. We don't have a Colonel Sanders. But I know that if we did, it would go over very well."

We asked her if there was an EST or an Arica Institute or any other kind of consciousness-raising group there.

"What are those?" she asked.

We explained as clearly as we could what those are.

"Oh," she said in an overly polite tone of voice—a tone of voice (we remembered it from past conversations with this young woman) that she uses to people when she thinks they are being really silly, or going too far.

We asked if The Fonz was popular there.

"The Fonz," she said. "What's that?"

We told her that The Fonz was a popular character named Fonzie, in a popular American television show. We told her how he styled his hair and the kinds of fifties clothes he wears, and we showed her his thumbs-up gesture.

She brightened up at this and said, "Well, we haven't heard of him yet, but even if it takes years we'll know about him. We pick up all the really good, stylish American things."

—*October 25, 1976*

Notes and Comment

We've just received a message from a friend—a very young woman, born into a world of air transportation. She writes:

Half past ten at night on the first of January, 1977, at the Amtrak train station in Cleveland, waiting to catch the eleven-five to New York. But the eleven-five will be at least an hour late, so I join the rest of the roomful of travellers in cursing the people who run the trains. At twelve o'clock, the train actually arrives, and everyone tries to get on first and so possibly install herself or himself in a window seat. I manage to get a window seat, but my overhead light doesn't work and I am not able to read. For the first ten minutes that I am in my seat, the seat beside me remains vacant. I throw my coat in it, so that it will look as if the occupant just went for a stroll into another car, and then I put on a tremendous frown, hoping to look so unpleasant no one will say to me, "Is anybody sitting here?" This way, if I feel like it later on, I can curl up and sleep comfortably. My little ruse doesn't work: a young woman comes along and asks, "Is anybody sitting here?" She sits down, and I look out the window. It has been snowing for days, so there is much snow on the ground, and it is white and beautiful and the night is clear and beautiful. I look at the woman seated next to me. She has open on her lap a large textbook, and I can see that it has something to do with natural childbirth and progressive child care. The woman turns to me and asks me my destination. When I tell her, she says, "That's where I am going, too," and then "Do you know that it took them three hours to get from Toledo to Cleveland?" And, without knowing what the normal time is for getting from Toledo to Cleveland, I join her in criticizing the people who run the railroad.

At half past two in the morning, the train makes its first stop since leaving Cleveland—at Erie, Pennsylvania—and many people get off, but I don't see anyone boarding. From the train I can see nothing with color in Erie, Pennsylvania, except, in the distance, two glowing golden arches. The woman who was sitting next to me has gone off to find a double seat she can sleep in. I decide to walk around. The car ahead of mine is in complete darkness. All the blinds are drawn, and all the people are sound asleep. It is very snug and warm in this car. Later, the conductor tells me that the lights in this car don't work at all, whereas the heating works too well. I walk up to the dining car, which is four cars away and open only for lounging. There are two waiters in the dining car, and the moment they see me they start saying almost crude things to me. I am not flustered at all—I just look at them and start barking like a dog. They shut up and leave the car. To myself I say, "Those two men are lucky I am not God." The train, which is going much faster than before, seems to be the only thing alive at this early hour of the morning. I go back to my seat to try to sleep. I take a pillow from an overhead rack. The pillowcase is white, but it looks and feels exactly like Handi-Wipes. I fall asleep, and this is what wakes me up: a man going through the car saying over and over, in a singsong way, "First call for breakfast." I like the way he says this so much that I would like to be able to push a button and have that very man appear and say those very words whenever I want. This is the first time I can actually feel myself having a good time on the train. And then I remember how much I like trains: that I like trains because they seem to be one of the more civilized ways to travel with a lot of other people; that I like to say to people, "I'm going by train," just because of the way it sounds; and that being on a train makes me feel important, and the nice thing about this feeling of importance is that no one need ever know about it and so ruin it for me. I go off to have breakfast, and find waiting on me the two waiters who were so rude the night before. And now they are addressing me as "Ma'am" and "Miss." For breakfast, I want to have pancakes, but when I see that they are regular-size pancakes, and not the silver-dollar size, I order French toast. The French toast arrives—three huge triangular hunks of crustless bread soaked in eggs and milk and then deep-fried. I eat it, and in a way it is the worst French toast I have ever eaten and in a way it is the best French toast I have ever eaten. It is the worst French toast because it is just plain not good food. It is the best French toast because the time is half past seven in the morning and I am on a train that is on its way out of Buffalo and heading for New York.

I get to New York fourteen and a half hours after boarding in Cleveland. I know that people can go to Europe and transact business and return in that span, and I think that's very nice. But I have had a neat old time just sitting at the train window looking at snow-covered farmhouses, frozen rivers, and miles and miles of snow-covered roads as they went by. And I have enjoyed myself so much that at the end of my trip I forgive the people at Amtrak for not running the trains on time, for not having good food, for not having the nicest waiters, and for just generally not being on the ball, and the next time I go anywhere I want to go by train.

—January 17, 1977

Interests

❧✦❧

We have a friend, an easily excited young woman, who from time to time likes to develop an abnormally intense interest in the most normal people and things. We have known this young woman for years now, and we have noticed that the intense-interest span is brief. We have here a list of some of the things that have interested her:

Nu Grape soda.

The television commercials for the Hotel Collingwood, on West Thirty-fifth Street.

The television commercials for Lenny's Clam Bar, a restaurant in Queens.

Fat girls. (She said that she had heard a comedian say to an audience at the Apollo Theatre, in Harlem, "Ever notice how all fat girls think they are fine?" and that the audience, which was about seventy-five per cent fat girls, laughed and laughed.)

Margaritas.

Macadamia nuts.

Ginseng Bee Secretion, a questionable tonic made in Red China.

Circle skirts and saddle shoes.

Tom McGuane novels.

Ordering through the mail unusual household utensils she has seen advertised in women's magazines (such as a set of little gadgets that are useful only when dealing with lemons).

We got a call from this young woman the other day. She was much excited. She said, "I have just been to Macy's. I have been going to Macy's every day for the last two weeks. I am very big on Macy's. I mean, it's such a big store. They say it's the biggest department store in the world. And there are always lots of people there. Ordinary people. I am very big on ordinary people. I got interested in Macy's when I read somewhere that Queen Salote of the Tonga Islands attended Queen Elizabeth's coronation in 1953 wearing an outfit that came from the tall girls' shop at Macy's. And I got interested again when I read somewhere that President Tubman of Liberia had his plumbing furnished and installed by Macy's. I read that about two weeks ago. Since then, I have bought a bed there, and a peach-colored bed ruffle for it, and peach-colored pillowcases, and peach-colored sheets, and a peach-colored comforter. I love peach. Then I bought bath towels and wineglasses and water goblets and a set of knives for carving and pots and pans and a stereo set and an umbrella and straight-leg corduroy jeans and a leaf-green linen shirt made in France and huge mugs made in Italy and a Poly Hot-

Pot (in avocado green, which is another one of my favorite colors, and which used to be the most popular color in the country) for making tea in my office, and chicken and sheep cheese for a dinner party I was giving, and nightgowns, and then I got one of their credit cards, because I was out of money. But the thing I like most about this particular store is how everything I buy there is something I really need. I am the one person I know who doesn't have to participate in meatless days, because I am not doing anything, such as over-consuming, to unnecessarily deplete the world's natural resources."

We could have asked her to explain that last line of reasoning, but we had never asked this young woman to explain any of her intense interests or the reasons she gave us for them, and we had no intention of starting now.

"Of course," she went on, "they have things other than what I need, and I know where it all is. I know, for instance, exactly where girls' T-shirts are kept and where boys' T-shirts are kept. I know where to find ladies' undergarments, men's leisure suits, school clothes for boys, school clothes for girls. I also know that in a single year Macy's New York uses up sixty-nine hundred miles of poly twine, three thousand miles of gummed tape, nineteen hundred miles of Scotch Tape, eleven thousand miles of packing tissue, twenty-five million paper bags, and five million gift boxes. Also, I know that Mr. Macy was a whaler from Nantucket before he decided to start selling things."

—*May 16, 1977*

Charm

For the last twenty-nine years, Ophelia DeVore, through her Ophelia DeVore School of Charm, has taught thousands of young black women how to do just about everything properly. She has given them lessons in Essentials of Good Grooming, Social Graces, Visual Poise, The First Step into an Adventure of Loveliness, Positive Thinking, Microphone Technique, and Figure Control with Fencing and Ballet. She has had some famous successes. Diahann Carroll, the singer-actress, is a graduate of the Ophelia DeVore School of Charm. So is the WABC newscaster Melba Tolliver. The actress Cicely Tyson used to be an instructor.

We recently visited Miss DeVore at the school, which is in midtown Manhattan, for a chat and a tour. She greeted us with a cheery "Hi!" A strikingly beautiful woman, with a smile that is both ready and winning, she wore a smartly tailored blue suit, a brown blouse, a brown scarf with blue dots, gold earrings, two gold rings on each hand, and brown shoes. Miss

DeVore told us, "I started out as a model in New York in 1946, when I was sixteen years old, and then it was very hard for a black girl. In 1946, there were very few good, sophisticated career jobs for the black girl. In 1947, I started doing this. I had my first class in a photographer's studio in Queens. I rented the space. Then I fixed up the basement of the house my parents and I were living in, in Queens, and I became so successful that in 1950 I had to move in to Manhattan. I had my whole family working for me. My husband was doing one thing, my children were doing others. I became an adviser to industry. I had to tell them how to use blacks without offending whites. I had to create from scratch, because there was no place for me to go to find out. I created fashion shows and beauty contests for my girls, so that they could get some experience in how to handle themselves. I made them feel special. At some point, all this will become extinct. As black people integrate, they won't want to do the special little things that they needed to do in an earlier time to get them across."

Miss DeVore showed us a big black book that was filled with photographs and newspaper clippings of her and of some of her famous students. Some of the photographs had captions. We saw a picture of Diahann Carroll. It had a caption that read, "At fifteen years of age, Miss Carroll came under the Influence of the Magic Touch of Miss DeVore." We saw a picture of Miss DeVore modelling nylons. We saw a picture of Melba Tolliver modelling baby-doll pajamas. We saw a picture of LaJeune Hundley, who at the Cannes Film Festival in 1960 became the second black girl (Cecelia Cooper was the first, in 1959) to win the title of Miss Festival.

Next, Miss DeVore took us into a classroom, where two small girls were being instructed in wardrobe planning as part of a Little Ladies course. They were learning to tell the difference between Lounge Wear, Sportswear, Dressy, Casual, and Formal. Then we sat in on a class for older girls. They were studying Good Grooming and Health, and displayed much enthusiasm. Then we sat in on Makeup III—Corrective. The women in this class were studying when to highlight and when to shadow parts of the face. The teacher, Mrs. Phyllis Branford, told them how to get "the hungry look" ("Highlight the cheekbones, shadow the jawbone"), how to slim the nose, and how to put on makeup for the stage. "Girls, remember," she said. "Mascara is a must, must, must."

—*June 6, 1977*

Garland Jeffreys

❧

We have just had two enjoyable encounters with Garland Jeffreys, a thirty-four-year-old New York songwriter and performer. The first was at a concert in Alice Tully Hall, at Lincoln Center. We had heard his recordings—particularly a song called "Wild in the Streets"—but had never seen him perform. He came onstage wearing black pants and a tailored gray pin-striped jacket (he removed it during the performance), a black T-shirt, and a tan Stetson hat. He danced around the stage for about five minutes before singing anything. The audience stood up and cheered him. He danced on as if unconscious of the cheers. Then he started to sing. He sang songs—all of them his own compositions—about New York, about his mother and father, about interracial love, about growing up in New York, about his own efforts to succeed as a songwriter, about teen-age rebellion, and about politics. He sang some of the songs to a rock-and-roll beat and some to a reggae beat. Whatever beat he used, he used it very well, and we came away from the concert feeling pleased and excited.

A few days after this, Garland Jeffreys invited us to drive out with him to Sheepshead Bay, in Brooklyn. He grew up there, and he wanted to show us part of his old neighborhood. He picked us up in a big black car, and he told the driver to go by the Belt Parkway. We got our first closeup look at Garland Jeffreys. He is a light-skinned black man with gray-green eyes and curly brown hair. On this occasion, he was wearing black pants, a regular black shirt, a blue plaid tie, and the same jacket and hat that he had worn onstage. He said to us, "I'm going to take you by my high school. I went to Abraham Lincoln High School. Then I'm going to take you by my house. We can't go in, though. My folks aren't in town. They're taking a trip across the country in a car. My folks are named Carmen and Ray. They are the nicest people."

On the Belt Parkway, just before we reached the exit to the Abraham Lincoln High School, we saw some children playing baseball. He said, "I used to play ball right here when I was little. I was a member of the Saint Mark's Little League. I played ball here from the time I was eight. My father was a great baseball player."

Then we came to the school. We saw some people dressed in various sports uniforms standing around the grounds. "I ran track here," he said.

"Were you any good?" we asked.

"No," he said, and he laughed. "There were always cats there who were faster than me."

We drove up to the front of the school. It looked like many pictures of American high schools. He looked around and said, "Things have really changed around here. See all these apartment buildings?" He pointed to some apartment buildings just across the street from the school. "Well, they were not here. There wasn't anything around here except a little candy store across the corner. Oh, hell, let's go on."

Garland Jeffreys directed the driver to go on to Brighton Beach. He wanted to pass by a billiard parlor where he used to play billiards, and he wanted to stop off at Irving's Delicatessen, where he and his friends used to buy sandwiches after they were through playing billiards. At the delicatessen, he bought some meats—corned beef and brisket—and potato salad, and some celery tonic, and we ate them in the car.

As we drove on, he said, "Do you see that sign?" We looked at a sign that said "Brighton Beach—Private." He said, "When I was little, I used to wonder why my friends could go into that place and I couldn't. I didn't know what was going on. I used to do everything I could to get into that place. But just look at it. It's a nothing place. I didn't know that then."

We drove to a section of Brighton Beach where there were some prosperous-looking houses. He said, "I used to come to this part of town three times a year. Trick-or-treating, Happy Thanksgiving, and shovelling snow."

Then we drove to Sheepshead Bay and passed a restaurant called Lundy's. He said that his grandfather had been the headwaiter there in the twenties and thirties and that his two uncles and his father had worked there as waiters. We drove by another restaurant, called Pips, where he said he himself used to be a waiter when he was a teen-ager. We drove by a Roman Catholic church, and he said he and his family were its only black members. We drove by a store where he said he bought his first tropical fish. We drove by a drugstore called Kips, where he said he had been a delivery boy. We drove by Ethel's Shop, where he said his mother bought her clothes. We drove by Bay Florist, where he said he had bought his mother flowers for Mother's Day when he was a boy. And we drove by a restaurant called Subway Hero Sandwiches, where he said he and his dad used to stop by for a hamburger and French fries when it was called the Yankee Diner.

Then we drove up to the house he grew up in. It is a nice, comfortable-looking three-story red brick house. It was late afternoon, and all the other houses looked busy with dinner-time. He reminded us that his parents were driving across the country. He said, "I can't go in. When I left home, they took my keys away." He laughed. Then he said, "I love this house now, but when I was growing up I used to wonder how come we couldn't live in an apartment. I used to want to live in an apartment so bad. When I was real little, I used to leave from here early in the morning and go to the schoolyard. I was for-ever in the schoolyard. I used to be playing ball, getting a sandwich at the corner, and then hanging out with my friends. We used to sing a lot. My favorite song to sing was called 'The Huckle Buck.' That was my song."

After this, we ran into some friends of his parents. They

embraced Jeffreys. They told him that his mother is very proud of him and that she speaks of him all the time. They also told him that ever since his parents went away all their friends have been regularly receiving postcards with amusing anecdotes about their trip. He said, "Yeah, I get postcards, too," and he removed from his jacket pocket a postcard from his parents. It said, "Hi!!! We spent 2½ weeks in Houston with Ray and Cora. Had a very nice time there. We are leaving Dallas on way to El Paso. Will get in touch soon. Give love to Carole. Love, Mom and Dad."

—July 11, 1977

Nothing in Mind

A young woman who lives in Chelsea writes:

I have a friend who comes from the Midwest, and he is very upset about two things: that soon most cars may come only in economy size, and that soon he may not be able to afford the gasoline even for these economy-size cars. My friend likes to drive around for no reason at all in a big car that uses up a lot of gasoline. When he gets into his car and drives off, he isn't going to the hospital to visit a friend, or going to the beach for a day of swimming and sunning, or going to the shopping mall to do some shopping, or even going somewhere to see some historic natural wonder. When he gets into his car and drives off, he heads for a highway; then, when he is far enough away from the city, he finds a less travelled back road, and then he drives and drives at about fifty miles an hour for hours; then he takes another road back to the highway and he comes home. My friend calls this cruising. Sometimes he will say to me, "I'm going cruising. Wanna come?" I always say yes. I like to do it, too, but I would never get up by myself and go off in a car with no destination in mind.

When my friend goes cruising, he takes with him a six-pack of Schaefer beer in the party-bottles size and an eight-pack of Miller beer in the pony size. The beer is always very cold. He takes these particular brands of beer because he has noticed that these are favorites among the Spanish-speaking people on the block where he lives. He keeps remarking about the difference between these people and the people he's seen in the television commercials for Miller and Schaefer beer. In the car, he never speaks except to swear at a careless motorist, or to point out something that is interesting to him and that he thinks will interest me, too. He turns on the car radio or puts a tape in the tape deck the moment he gets into the car, and the music is never off until he gets home again. He sits behind the wheel with his legs slightly apart, his right foot on the accelerator, the leg crooked at the knee and resting sidewise on the seat, his right hand looking as if it were casually holding the wheel, his left hand on the armrest. He can afford to look this relaxed because the car has power steering.

When I am in the car with my friend, I think of other times I have been in cars with people just for the fun of driving. When I was little, my mother would say, "We are taking a motorcar trip to . . ." and she would name some place hours away from where we were. Then we would pile into the car and drive to the place and turn right around and come home again. At the time, my mother was in love with religious music, especially if it was sung by Jim Reeves, and she would turn the car radio to a radio station that played religious music, mostly sung by Jim Reeves. On the night of my sixteenth birthday, my godmother and her husband took me for a drive in their gray Hillman (an English car), and on the car radio I heard the disc jockey say that my mother had requested that "Happy Birthday Sweet Sixteen," by Neil Sedaka, be played in honor of me. I didn't know what to make of it, hearing my name on the radio, but what was worse was that my mother would think that just because I liked rock and roll I liked Neil Sedaka. Then, when I was in my early twenties, I had a boyfriend who would take me for long drives in the country, and while we were driving he would play over and over, on the tape-deck machine, the song "A Whiter Shade of Pale," by Procol Harum. Afterward, we would go to bars that had electric-blue-lighted jukeboxes. I have known, in fact, many boys who like to drive around and listen to tapes or to the radio and drink beer. I have never known any girls who did this. Not even one.

My friend from the Midwest has told me about some of his driving adventures. He says that he once drove around the state of Wyoming with a friend for five days with only eight dollars between them, plus his friend's father's oil-company credit card. He says that the state of Wyoming is the best for driving. He says that he knows every driving inch of the old logging roads in the state of Michigan. He says that driving around in the summer in an air-conditioned Buick in the flatness that is Nebraska is the only boring thing he has found to be a complete pleasure. He says that stretches of Ohio were made for driving around with nothing in mind. It is the memory of these things that makes him hate a future of economy cars and gasoline shortages. He curses the modern age and people with too many children. In the meantime, he continues to drive around for no reason at all in his big car that uses up a lot of gasoline. Just the other night, a nice summer evening, we went for a drive up around the Woodstock area. Suddenly, on the car radio we heard "I Heard It Through the Grapevine," by Marvin Gaye. My friend turned to me and he smiled, because he knows that I know that this is one of his super-favorite driving songs. At the end of the song, he turned around and we came home.

—July 18, 1977

Notes and Comment

A young woman we know writes:

I grew up on an island in the West Indies which has an area of a hundred and eight square miles. On the island were many sugarcane fields and a sugar-making factory and a factory where both white and dark rum were made. There were cotton fields, but there were not as many cotton fields as there were sugarcane fields. There were arrowroot fields and tobacco fields, too, but there were not as many arrowroot fields and tobacco fields as there were cotton fields. Some of the fifty-four thousand people who lived on the island grew bananas and mangoes and eddoes and dasheen and christophine and sweet potatoes and white potatoes and plums and guavas and grapes and papaws and limes and lemons and oranges and grapefruits, and every Saturday they would bring them to the market, which was on Market Street, and they would sell the things they had grown. This was the only way many of them could make a living, and, though it sounds like farming, they weren't farmers in the way a Mid-western wheatgrower is a farmer, and they didn't think of the plots of land on which they grew these things as The Farm. Instead, the plots of land were called The Ground. They might say, "Today, me a go up ground." The Ground was often many miles away from where they lived, and they got there not by taking a truck or some other kind of automotive trans-portation but by riding a donkey or by walking. A small num-ber—a very small number—of the fifty-four thousand people worked in banks or in offices. The rest of them—the ones who didn't grow the things that were sold in the market on Saturdays or work in the factories or the fields, the banks or the offices—were carpenters or masons or servants in the new hotels for tourists which were appearing suddenly all over the island, or servants in private homes, or seamstresses, or tailors, or shopkeepers, or fishermen, or dockworkers, or schoolchildren. All of these different people doing all these different things did this one thing: they were all up and about by half past five in the morning, and they did this without the help of an alarm clock or an automatic clock radio. Every morning—workday, Saturday, or Sunday—the whole island was alive by six o'clock. People got up early on weekdays to go to work or to school; they got up early on Saturday to go to market; and they got up early on Sunday to go to church.

It is true that the early morning is the most beautiful time of day on the island. The sun has just come up and is imme-diately big and bright, the way the sun always is on an island, but the air is still cool from the night; the sky is a deep, cool blue (like the sea, it gets lighter as the day wears on, and then it gets darker, until by midnight it looks black); the red in the hibiscus and the flamboyant flowers seems redder; the green of the trees and grass seems greener. If it is December, there is dew everywhere: dew on the painted red galvanized rooftops; dew on my mother's upside-down washtubs; dew on the stones that make up her stone heap (a round mound of big and little stones in the middle of our yard; my mother spreads out soapy white laundry on these stones, so that the hot sun will bleach them even whiter); dew on the vegetables in my mother's treasured (to her, horrible to me) vegetable garden. But it wasn't to admire any of these things that people got up so early. I had never, in all the time I lived there, heard anyone say, "What a beautiful morning." Once, just the way I had read it in a book, I stretched and said to my mother, "Oh, isn't it a really lovely morning?" She didn't reply to that at all, but she pulled my eyelids this way and that and then said that my sluggish liver was getting even more sluggish. I don't know why people got up so early, but I do know that they took great pride in this. It wasn't unusual at all to hear one woman say to another, "Me up since way 'fore day mornin'," and for the other woman to say back to her, with a laugh, "Yes, my dear, you know de early bird ketch de early worm."

In our house, we got up every day at half past five. This is what got us up: every morning, Mr. Jarvis—a dockworker who lived with his wife (she sold sweets she had made herself to schoolchildren at the bus depot just before they boarded buses that would take them back to their homes in the country) and their eight children in a house at the very end of our street—would take his herd of goats to pasture. At exactly half past five, he and his goats reached our house. We heard the cries of the goats and the sound the stake at the end of the chain tied around their necks made as it dragged along the street. Above the sound of what my mother called "that early morning racket," we could hear Mr. Jarvis whistling. Mostly, he whistled the refrain of an old but popular calypso tune. The words in the refrain were "Come le' we go, Soukie, Come le' we go." If we heard only the crying of the goats and the sound of their chain, we knew that it was Mr. Jarvis's son Nigel, a rude wharf-rat boy, who was taking the goats to pasture.

We weren't the only ones who got up to the sound of Mr. Jarvis and his goats. Mr. Gordon, a man who grew lettuce and sold most of it to the new hotels and who lived right next to us, would get up soon after Mr. Jarvis passed. He would throw open all the windows and all the doors in his house, and he would turn on his radio and tune it to a station in St. Croix, a station which at that hour played American country-and-Western music. It may have been from this that my mother developed her devotion to the music of Hank Williams. Mr. Gordon was very nice to my family, but that didn't prevent me from deciding that he resembled a monkey, and so I nicknamed him Monkey Lettuce. I called him this only behind his and my parents' back, of course. We never tuned our radio to the station in St. Croix. Instead, at exactly seven o'clock, my parents turned on our radio and tuned it to the station on our island. A man's voice would say, "It is seven o'clock." Then another voice, a completely different voice, would say, "This is the BBC, London." Then we would listen to the news being broadcast. At around that time, we sat down to eat breakfast.

Between the time I got up and eight o'clock, I would have helped my mother fill her washtubs with water, swept up the yard, fed the chickens, taken a bath in cold water, polished my shoes, pressed my school uniform (gray pleated-linen tunic, pink poplin blouse), gone to the grocer (Mr. Richards) to buy fresh bread (two fourpence loaves, one each for my mother and father; a twopence loaf for me; and three penny loaves, one each for my little brothers) and also to buy butter and cheese (made in New Zealand), gone to Miss Roma to have my hair freshly braided, and eaten a breakfast of porridge, eggs, bread and butter, cheese, and hot Ovaltine. By that time, it was no longer early morning on our island, and half an hour later, together with two hundred and ninety-nine other girls and three hundred boys, I would be in my school auditorium singing, "All things bright and beautiful, All creatures great and small."

I now live in Manhattan. The only thing it has in common with the island where I grew up is a geographical definition. Certainly no one I know gets up at half past five, at six o'clock, at half past six, at seven o'clock, at half past seven, at eight o'clock. I know one person who sleeps all day and stays up all night. I know another person who has to take a nap if he gets up before noon. And how easy it is, I have noticed, to put a great distance between you and a close friend if you should call that friend before ten in the morning.

I wake up, still, without an alarm, at half past five. In the neighborhood in which I live, it is very quiet at that hour. It is not romantic at all to hear nothing in the city. At around six o'clock, I begin to hear the sound of moving vehicles. Trucks. I know they are trucks because the sound I hear is a rumbling sound that only trucks make. The sound sometimes comes from streets far away. If I get up and look out, I might not see anyone. If I see anyone, it is almost always two or three men together, dressed identically, in tight black leather pants, a black leather jacket, a black leather cap, and black leather boots. They will walk very quickly down my street as if they are in a great hurry. When I look out, I never notice the early light playing on the street or on the brownstone houses across the street from me. In Manhattan, I notice only whether it is sunny and bright or cloudy and gray or raining or snowing. I never notice things like gradations of light, but my friends tell me that they are there.

Between six and seven, I sit and read women's magazines. I read articles about Elizabeth Taylor's new, simple life, articles about Mary Tyler Moore, articles about Jane Pauley, articles about members of the Carter family, articles about Candice Bergen, articles about Doris Day, articles about Phyllis Diller, and excerpts from Lana Turner's autobiography. I know many things about these people—things that they may have forgotten themselves and things that, should we ever meet, they might wish I would forget also. At seven o'clock, I watch the morning news for one whole hour. I watch the morning news for two reasons: it makes me feel as if I am living in Chicago, and on the morning news I see and hear the best reports on anything having to do with pigs. I don't know why the morning news makes me feel as if I am living in Chicago and not, say, Cleveland, but there it is. I love Chicago and would like to live there, but only for an hour. Some days, after watching the morning news, my head is filled with useless (to me) but interesting information about pigs. Some of the information, though, is good only for a day. Then, for half an hour, I watch Captain Kangaroo. I love Captain Kangaroo and have forgiven him for saying to Chastity Bono, when they were both guests on her parents' television show, "Now, let me lay this on you, Chastity." Surely a grown man, even if he is a children's hero (perhaps because he is a children's hero), shouldn't talk like that.

Then it is half past eight and no longer early morning in Manhattan, either.

—*October 17, 1977*

Notes and Comment

✦

We have a letter from an excitable young woman we know:

I've just returned from a party given to celebrate the publication of a book, edited by Linda Rosen Obst, that is called
The Sixties. The subtitle is "The Decade Remembered Now,
By the People Who Lived It Then." I took a look at it. It's a
great book—especially if you only look at the pictures. My favorite picture is one with Muhammad Ali holding Ringo Starr
aloft in his arms as if he—Muhammad Ali—were a butcher
and Ringo Starr were a leg of mutton. The other Beatles are
in the picture, too. My favorite article, by Wavy Gravy, is on
the Woodstock music festival. It made me glad I wasn't
there—particularly since I didn't want to go. My favorite title
for an article in the book is "Dylan Goes Electric." To that I
would like to say, "Yes, and thousands cheered." But here's the
thing about the party for the book. It was held in a sort of
high-toned discothèque called New York, New York. I heard
many people say that this was a huge irony, because when

you think of what the sixties meant and what discothèques mean you reach the conclusion that the sixties and discothèques are horses of such different colors. But actually I thought that the people who gave the party (Random House) provided some nice sixties touches. For one thing, there was a full bar and you didn't have to pay for any of the drinks you ordered. For another, there wasn't anybody to take your coat and you had to plop it down in an alcove that was reserved for coats, so there were all these coats in an alcove and if you had a particular nice and favorite coat you just had to leave it and trust that no one would take it. I thought that the leave-it-and-trust part was very sixties. For another thing, they played "Purple Haze" at least once. In fact, they played many songs by groups from the sixties, but not many people danced to them. There were about three hundred people at the party, and I saw six people dancing to "Sympathy for the Devil." When it was followed by "Love Is the Message," a disco song by the MFSB Orchestra, the whole dance floor got very crowded. I also heard a group of people talking about Punk Rock and New Wave music, and they talked about it as if it were really important, but I couldn't figure out if Punk Rock and New Wave were the same thing or two completely different things. Anyway, one man said he liked the energy in New Wave music, even though the politics of New Wave music was offensive. I am sure that in years to come he will write an article about New Wave music that has as stop-the-presses a title as "Dylan Goes Electric." Later, a woman told me that all those people talking about Punk Rock and New Wave were rock-and-roll critics. She said, "Do you know how Mick Jagger said that he didn't want to be forty-five and singing 'Satisfaction'? Well, worse than that is being forty-five and writing about Mick Jagger singing 'Satisfaction.'" I laughed. That is the only funny thing I heard anyone say at the party the whole evening.

—January 16, 1978

Pippo

✦

One recent morning, we noticed an advertisement at the Forty-second Street station of the Sixth Avenue subway. The advertisement was for a beauty salon called Pippo of Rome. It said "WE MAKE EVERYONE LOOK THEIR BEST!" and "14 INTERNA- TIONALLY FAMOUS HAIRCUTTERS. ALL UNDER THE PERSONAL SU- PERVISION OF PIPPO OF ROME." After peace and justice, there is nothing in the world we like more than for everyone to look his or her best, and, after some of Richard Pryor's jokes, there is almost nothing we find funnier than Internationally Fa- mous Haircutters and any noun followed by the words "of Rome." Encountering the advertisement, therefore, impelled us to visit Pippo of Rome, which proved to be a unisex beauty salon. We met Pippo himself—Mr. Pippo Guastella—and thought he was great. He looked like pictures we remem- bered seeing some years ago of Carlo Ponti, the Italian film producer who is now married to Sophia Loren. Pippo was dressed in sky blue: pants, shirt, and sweater all exactly the same shade. He introduced us to some of the internationally known hairdressers. He told us that he had studied hairdressing in Rome and had worked there in a shop on the Via Veneto; that he had worked in Rome for a man called Frank the Neapolitan; that Cary Grant, Gregory Peck, Rosalind Russell, the President of Italy, and other famous people used to have their hair done at Frank the Neapolitan's place; that he himself had twice given Gregory Peck a haircut; that he had come to New York because everybody comes to New York; that he had opened his first salon in New York in 1959 and by 1960 it had taken off; and that he changed the furniture in his salon every two years. The furniture that he now has is in the Chesterfield style.

Pippo then showed us an Italian men's magazine called UOMO. As he showed us pictures of snappily dressed men with precision-styled hair, he said, "In Italy, it's different from here. As you know, there is a lot of art over there, and this makes everybody—hairdressers, designers—very conscious of personality. When a customer comes in, you take everything into consideration. Face, personality—everything. I get all Italian magazines, because they keep me on top of things. In America, everybody wants to look the same. Same haircut, same clothes. But I give all my customers something different, to fit their personalities. I used to do the hair of Joe Franklin. You know, his face is puffed out like this!" Pippo made a face like a balloon, and then made a sound like air escaping from a balloon. "He would wear his hair flat on top, making him look even puffier. So I styled his hair so that he

looks all slimmed down. He's a very nice man. Then, I do
Barry Farber. He is more philosophic, and these philosophers
don't take care of themselves. I first saw him as a judge in a
Miss America pageant. He was wearing a nice suit and he
looked nice, but his hair was a mess. Then, one day, I see him
in the lobby of the WOR building and I tell him what I think
of him, and since then he has been coming to me to do his
hair. In other words, I brought out his personality. A long time
ago, I styled the hair of Tony Lo Bianco, but then he went to
Hollywood. Now I style his brother John's hair."

We watched Pippo wash and style a man's hair. He had introduced the man to us as a special and long-standing customer. Pippo washed the man's hair once with a shampoo
called Superstar Professional Shampoo. Then he cut the hair
by dividing it up into very small sections and cutting off a half
inch or so. Then he massaged the man's scalp, fluffed up his
hair, and trained some hair-drying lamps on it. After Pippo
was done, the man looked just like a celebrity on local television.

—*March 6, 1978*

Honors

One miserable afternoon last week (it was the weather, and it was raining), we went to a great party for J. Barney Ferguson, who was this year's Grand Marshal for this year's St. Patrick's Day Parade. Here are some of the things that made it great: It was held in a really big room, and this really big room was filled up, mostly, with big, flush-faced gentlemen, not one of them wearing a leisure suit, and all of them holding a glass of whiskey and telling each other what sounded, from the laughs, like really funny jokes; the real name of the guest of honor, J. Barney Ferguson, is James Bernard Ferguson, and he is a policeman, in homicide; we saw two priests in the room, and, except for their priests' clothes, they were just as flush-faced and just as jovial as the other gentlemen. J. Barney Ferguson wore a gray pin-striped suit, a white shirt, and a green-and-gold striped tie. He has a good grip of a handshake and a big smile. We liked him, and so did all the other people in the room. They all went up to him, exchanged anecdotes with him, and told him jokes. He laughed a lot. Then a number of

these people lined up to have their picture taken with J. Barney
Ferguson. Patrick Cunningham, Bronx County Democratic
Chairman, had his picture taken with J. Barney Ferguson; the
editor Dennis Flanagan had his picture taken with J. Barney
Ferguson; Monsignor Jack Barry, who is a monsignor with the
Police Department, had his picture taken with J. Barney Ferguson; Michael Maye, the former president of the Uniformed
Firefighters Association, had his picture taken with J. Barney
Ferguson (Michael Maye was wearing the best loud jacket of
any loud jacket we have ever seen—it was red-and-gray big
plaid); William Twomey, an inspector with the City Department
of Consumer Affairs, had his picture taken with J. Barney Ferguson; two people from Rumm's, a tavern in Manhattan, had
their picture taken with J. Barney Ferguson; Jerry Fitzgerald, a
policeman and J. Barney Ferguson's partner on the squad, had
his picture taken with J. Barney Ferguson; Denis Carey, of the
Red Blazer Pub, had his picture taken with J. Barney Ferguson;
John Keenan, New York State's Special Prosecutor, had his picture taken with J. Barney Ferguson; and John and William Ferguson, foremen with the New York City Highway Department
and J. Barney Ferguson's brothers, had their picture taken with
J. Barney Ferguson. This was a five-to-seven party, and at
around half past six people started to make speeches about
what a great man J. Barney Ferguson really is. Then they gave
him, as a token of their appreciation, a beautiful walking stick.
This seemed like a good idea and a good gift, because J. Barney
Ferguson has three broken bones in his back. It happened last
year while he was chasing a murder suspect.

—*March 27, 1978*

Dinosaurs

❧

This is one of the nicest things to do in New York on a Sunday afternoon: Have a good late breakfast (something like a bowl of porridge, some scrambled eggs, some smoked herring, toast with raspberry jam would be just fine), and then put on some comfortable clothes and some comfortable shoes and go over to the American Museum of Natural History. If there are children in your family, by all means take them along. While you are there, don't miss the redwood-tree exhibit in the Hall of North American Forests, the worm exhibit in the Hall of the Biology of Invertebrates, the early-man exhibit in the Hall of the Biology of Man, the Mbuti Pygmies of the Ituri Forest in the Hall of Man in Africa, and the bird-watching exhibit in the Akeley Gallery. This is just what we did on a recent Sunday afternoon. We saw all the things we liked best and then a few of the things that are interesting anyway. It was while we were looking at a few of the things that are interesting anyway that we came across, in progress, a lecture on dinosaurs. The lecture was being given by Sidney Horenstein, a paleontologist on the museum's staff, and was sponsored by the New York Paleontological Society. Sitting on some yellow petroleum-by-product chairs, listening closely to him, and watching some slides he showed to accompany his chat were lots of moms and dads and their little children. Some other little children were in strollers. Mr. Horenstein said that dinosaurs were around two hundred and ten million years ago; that at that time the earth's atmosphere was warm; that as a group they lasted for one hundred and fifty million years, compared to our (man's) measly two million; that most dinosaurs were plant-eaters except a few, like the great *Tyrannosaurus rex*, which apparently ate smaller dinosaurs; that one bite for a *T. rex* could probably feed a human family of four for one month; that the *Megalosaurus* was the first dinosaur to be described scientifically; that the word "dinosaur" means "terrible lizard"; that dinosaurs that had lost their teeth stole dinosaur eggs and ate them; that *T. rex* had small hands, and no one knows what purpose its hands served except that maybe after it slept its hands helped it get up; that one genus with a bony crest on its head was called *Kritosaurus*, which means "chosen lizard"; that maybe dinosaurs became extinct because an interstellar explosion caused the earth's atmosphere to cool and the dinosaurs died of exposure, but then again maybe their extinction was caused by something else; that no one has ever seen a dinosaur or knows what dinosaurs really did. While Mr. Horenstein talked, he showed slides of dinosaurs doing things, and almost always the dinosaurs were in a swamp or near a swamp. He showed slides of dinosaurs with long, swanlike necks. He showed slides of baby dinosaurs just emerging from eggs the size of large avocados. He showed slides of dinosaurs attacking egg-stealing dinosaurs. He showed slides of dinosaurs eating no-longer-alive dinosaurs. He showed slides of dinosaurs with big teeth and slides of dinosaurs with little teeth. He showed slides of dinosaurs whose mouths looked like duck bills, and said that these dinosaurs were called hadrosaurs (meaning "bulky lizards"). He showed slides of dinosaurs with two horns and slides of dinosaurs with just one horn. He showed a slide of two dinosaurs battering their heads together. He showed slides of pink dinosaurs, blue dinosaurs, and green dinosaurs. Mr. Horenstein made it clear that it would be just wonderful to be one of these creatures, standing around in a gooey, warm swamp with your friends.

—*April 24, 1978*

Kenya

❧✦❧

Kenya is the most beautiful place in the world. Some of the first men and women to live on this earth lived in Kenya. Kenya lies on the equator, but most of it is a high plateau—an ideal atmosphere for all kinds of plants, animals, and people. Early Stone Age Kenyans were hunters and gatherers. The Dorobo, a tribe of people who live in Kenya, think that they in particular are the descendants of the first men and women who lived in Kenya. The great Masai tribesmen, who live on the plateau, are interested mainly in raising cattle and fighting wars to get more cattle. The Kikuyu are the largest tribe in Kenya. The Mau Mau mostly belonged to the Kikuyu tribe. The great explorer Vasco da Gama was probably the first European in Kenya, though possibly the Greeks were there in the first century. Da Gama landed at Mombasa in 1498. The great railroad in Kenya that runs from Mombasa to Lake Victoria was built between 1895 and 1901; it cost the British government over five million pounds. It was built mostly by

Indians from India, and lions ate twenty-eight of the builders near the Tsavo River Bridge. Johann Ludwig Krapf and Johannes Rebmann, two German missionaries, were the first white men to see interior Kenya. In 1848, Rebmann was the first white man to see Mount Kilimanjaro, which is now in Tanzania. In 1849, Krapf was the first white man to see Mount Kenya. Charles Millet, of Salem, Massachusetts, was the first American trading captain to visit Mombasa. This was in 1827, and his ship was named *Ann*. There are thirteen million people in Kenya. It is almost the size of Texas. In Kenya, you can buy a Reuben sandwich, a boneless steak, or lobster thermidor in a restaurant.

We learned all this from a man—a Kenyan—at the first Kenya Trade Fair, which we visited while it was at the Coliseum. As he talked, we walked about looking at stalls displaying goods made in Kenya. We saw a stall displaying coffee beans, roasted and unroasted. We saw a stall displaying three different kinds of tea. We saw many stalls displaying wood or stone carvings of animals, birds, trees, and people. We saw the stall of Ideal Farm, the largest mushroom grower in black Africa. We saw the stall of Kenya Orchards, producers of fruit juice and jam. We saw the stall of the House of Manji, Ltd., makers of Buitoni pasta in Kenya. We saw a stall displaying canned corned beef and canned ox tongue. We learned that in Kenya there is a brand of cooking fat called Cowboy. It comes in a can, too, and the label on the can is a photograph of an incredibly handsome and incredibly black man wearing a white cowboy hat. We learned that Lady Gay is a brand of talcum powder and that Tusker is a locally made beer. Then we saw a fashion show. In the fashion show were many styles of clothing that can be found in any old store, such as a bikini, a suit, pants, and dresses, but then there were other, very fine-looking garments—all different ways to wear a bright-colored, boldly patterned sheet. From everything in the fashion show, we could see that it has never occurred to the average Kenyan to dress up in clothes that could in any way be called demure.

—*June 5, 1978*

Cheese

At a luncheon the Dorman Cheese Company gave the other day, at the Sky Garden Roof of the St. Moritz, in honor of Mary Anne Krupsak, the Lieutenant Governor of New York; Carol Bellamy, the New York City Council President; John Lindsay, the former Mayor of New York City; Lewis Rudin, an influential New York real-estate man; Alan King, the comedian; and Sandy, a dog and a star in the Broadway musical *Annie*—because the Dorman Cheese Company thinks they are all good New Yorkers—here are some of the people and things we saw and heard:

Alan King wearing a brown herringbone sports jacket. Carol Brock, a food columnist for the *News*. Avram Dorman, the president of Dorman Cheese. Carol Dorman, the wife of Avram Dorman. William Dorman, vice-president of Dorman Cheese. Phyllis Dorman, William Dorman's wife, wearing a roomy maroonish dress. Jeff and Ned Dorman, their sons. Carol Bellamy wearing a smartly tailored blue suit. Alice

Weiss, Phyllis Dorman's friend from Scarsdale. Carol Bellamy sipping water. John Lindsay buttering bread, then eating the buttered bread. Sandy the dog wearing a black bow tie and lapping up water from a water glass. Phyllis Dorman saying, when she saw Sandy the dog lapping up the water from the water glass, "Oh, my God!"

Also: Phyllis Dorman saying to a woman she had just met, "I am from Charleston, West Virginia. I married Billy twenty-seven years ago, and today is our anniversary." Phyllis Dorman saying to a man, "Herman, is Susie here?" Phyllis Dorman saying to the people at her table, "Could we make some room for Herman? Move over a little." Sandy the dog barking. Sandy the dog wearing a white napkin. Sandy the dog looking sad-eyed, the way all dogs look when they are around people eating. Phyllis Dorman calling out from her table to Alan King, who was sitting on the dais, "Alan, is your speech going to be better than Sandy's?"

Also: Alan King staring across the room past Phyllis Dorman's head. Phyllis Dorman's friend Alice saying to Phyllis Dorman, about the first-course antipasto, "This should be the whole lunch. It's so much and it's so good." Alice, as she watched Sandy eat up a large slice of cheese, saying, "Kay Thompson's dog ate pasta like that in Florence."

Also: William Dorman handing out awards—bronze wedges of Swiss cheese—to the good New Yorkers. Carol Bellamy sipping more water. Phyllis Dorman saying to her friend Alice, "Billy and I are going to Wimbledon on Sunday." Alice saying to Phyllis Dorman, "We played tennis with Jack Paar at his house in Connecticut. He has a little TV camera on the court that tapes the game as you play, and later he shows the tape. It's fun to see yourself." Phyllis Dorman saying, "Ugh, I can't bear to watch myself."

Also: Carol Bellamy, Alan King, John Lindsay, Lewis Rudin, and Sandy posing, with their awards, for photographers. John Lindsay leaving after lunch. Mary Anne Krupsak arriving after lunch. William Dorman telling an after-lunch joke about how much he hates photographers telling him to say "cheese" when they are taking his picture. William Dorman telling the roomful of people that it was his and Phyllis Dorman's twenty-seventh wedding anniversary, and then saying to Phyllis Dorman, "Here's to my big cheese," and holding out to her an award similar to the awards that the honored New Yorkers had received. Mrs. Dorman clasping her hands over her mouth and then saying, "Oh, that's so sweet."

—*July 3, 1978*

Notes and Comment

A letter from a young woman we know:

When I decided that the place I was living in was too small for me, I told everyone that I was moving. I would just say, "I am moving." I didn't know where I would move to, but I would say it anyway. I said it to my landlord. In a note to him, I said, "Dear Herb"—I can call him by his first name like that because he is a likable man and we are on good terms— "I am moving. The place here is too small." Weeks later, he called, and when he found out that I didn't have a place to move to after all, he rented me some space—much bigger and cheaper than what I had before. Only, it is in a funny part of town. I am now living in the spice district.

Two things women I know say are hard to find: a nice place to live and a nice man. Two things men and women I know say are hard to find: a good job and a good place to live. Two things a lot of people I know say they hate to do most, of all the things they hate to do: look for a place to live and then move into it.

My friend Rudy said that I should go to the liquor store at the end of the day and ask the people there for some of the boxes they keep in the back until the rubbish man comes. He was perfectly sure about it. He said that's how it always is at liquor stores—at the end of every day they have a lot of empty boxes waiting for the rubbish man. Then he gave me these instructions: Take four boxes and stack them up one on top of another and tie them together with a thick piece of string. Repeat with four more boxes. Pick them up and go home. Four boxes in each hand, eight boxes at a time. He said, "It will make you look like an old-time coolie." I went to the liquor store twice and brought back, altogether, sixteen boxes. Rudy went to the liquor store six times and brought back forty-eight. That added up to sixty-four: it took sixty-four boxes to hold all the things I own. Most of the things I own should be thrown away, but I can never throw away anything unless I am drunk.

It took Rudy three Monday nights, three Thursday nights, and two Saturday nights to put all my things in the sixty-four boxes. At the end of it, he said, "There. I hope you feel better now." Rudy works at a movie theatre where it costs a dollar to see a show. I used to go see films there, but that was before he told me in quite alarming detail about the mice who live there and what a racket they make during the shows. I think that if I go to the theatre the mice will turn out to be as big as people, and will want to sit next to me.

How miserable everything seemed. So it must be true what they say about moving, after all. I hated the woman who would be moving in after I moved out. I hated her even though I knew nothing about her to hate. She would call up and ask if she could come over to measure for curtains, bookshelves, space for pieces of furniture—this, that. Then I found out that she was a cellist, and out of work, too, so I softened. "How nice," I said. "A cellist." But still. The woman who lived there before me lived there for forty years. She moved out when she died. When I was getting ready to move out, I hated so many things. I hated the way some of the women I knew dressed up as if they were old men, in men's clothes that were baggy on them. I hated the way some of the women I knew dressed up as if they were little girls, in ankle socks and wearing their hair in little plaits, with schoolgirl ribbons at the ends. I hated everything around me.

As for the day I moved, everyone said what a cheery, sunny day it was, and what good, sound, careful, cheap movers I had. I didn't see it that way. I hated what I was doing, but here I was, doing it.

—*September 11, 1978*

Soap

At the First International Soap Opera Exposition, held in the Statler Hilton some days ago, we saw many stout middle-aged women with cameras and many stout middle-aged women with children. We saw five men who were there because they liked and watched soap operas; all the other men we saw were connected with the exposition. We sat in a room filled with some of the stout middle-aged women with cameras and the stout middle-aged women with children. On a dais in the room were three actresses and an actor who play leading roles in a soap opera. In the middle of the room was a microphone. The women lined up in an orderly way to ask the actresses and the actor questions. The women called the actresses and the actor by their soap-opera names.

Among the questions that the women asked the actresses and the actor were these:

"Is there ever a time when you get into a part so much that when you get home you can't get out of it?"

"Did you get married on Valentine's Day?"

"How do you get along off camera?"

"If you had to pick a part other than your own on your show, which part would it be?"

"Why can't you be honest with Pete and tell him you don't love him?"

"What do you like to do with your free time?"

"You are all so lovely and thin. How do you maintain your weight?"

"Are you married when you are not on the show?"

"How do you prepare yourself when you have to cry?"

One of the actresses said that Louis Malle was considering a screenplay she had written about Henri Christophe, one of the eighteenth-century liberators of Haiti. Another said she liked to have fun. The third said she liked life to be a blast. All three actresses said they had to watch the amount and kind of food they ate. All three actresses said that when they had a particularly difficult and emotional scene to do they tried to think of particularly difficult and emotional scenes in their own lives. All three actresses said they were not married. The actor announced that he was appearing in an Off Broadway show. The actor said that the Off Broadway show was a very *good* Off Broadway show, and that he hoped the people in the audience would come and see it. The three actresses laughed with the audience and with each other. The actor seemed serious and standoffish.

Just before the interview session was over, a woman stood up and said, "I watch your show every day. It's like a religious thing with me."

The whole room stood up and cheered.

—*September 18, 1978*

Collecting

Information gathered from press releases picked up at the World Plate Collectors Fair, recently held at the Statler Hilton:

"These are not plates to be eaten off, but to be admired, to be traded, to be acquired—often for surprisingly-large sums of money."

"Plate collecting bids fair to become THE investment vehicle of the 1980s."

"Between the two World Wars, the Christmas plate business waxed strong in Europe, and might never have spread to the United States had it not been for the returning G.I.s in 1945 and 1946."

"Demand for plates really began in 1969, when Bing & Grondahl issued its now famous 'Dog and Puppies' Mother's Day plate."

"What do artists Edna Hibel, Ted deGrazia, Mary Vickers, Dolores Valenza, James Wyeth, Leroy Neiman, Ole Winther,

John McClelland, and Prescott Baston have in common other than their oils, brushes, and canvas? They are all members of a revered pantheon of painters whose works are being bought up by plate collectors faster than you can say Leonardo da Vinci (who to the best of anyone's knowledge is not represented on any plate—yet)."

"New plate issues don't 'react' to world events like another threat from OPEC the way new stock issues do."

"John Wayne, Kate Smith, Muhammad Ali, and Betty Ford are avid plate collectors, as are 4.5 million other Americans."

"Rarity: Is the edition tightly limited yet not too limited to create a market? If the edition is closed, are dealers bidding in the secondary market? Collectibility: Is it one, preferably the first, of a collectible periodic series or merely a single issue? Time of Acquisition: Can you get it at the right time—at issue—or while the price is still rising? Sponsorship: Is it issued in association with a government or an official non-profit institution? Commemorative importance: Does it commemorate a seasonal event or a historic event? If so, does it bring new insight to the event? Or is it an event in the history of the artist or of the maker?"

We ourself saw plates with single flower, bouquet of flowers, old ships docked in Boston Bay, children playing in snow, woman holding child on knee, man holding child on knee, Judy Garland in *Wizard of Oz* dress, frog having dinner with a handsome man and a handsome woman, man mending clock, street scene in Paris, signs of the zodiac, Virgin Mary, Japanese women, ship caught in a fierce storm, blue jays resting on a tree branch, cardinals resting on a tree branch, Vivien Leigh as Scarlett O'Hara.

We saw no plates of incredible beauty, but we liked all plates that had illustrations by Norman Rockwell.

We can't see why people collect plates. Can't see why people collect anything.

—October 9, 1978

Memorandum

The other day, Mayor Koch acted as host at a lunch for Merv Griffin, because Merv Griffin's new contract calls for him to tape six weeks of his *Merv Griffin Show* here each year for the next five years. The Mayor said that this was a good thing for New York and one more sign that New York was on its way back up. Before lunch, which was to take place in the Blue Room at City Hall, people gathered in an upstairs room for cocktails. Merv Griffin himself, wearing gray pants and a navy jacket, and looking almost too well fed, told stories about Las Vegas to people who are in show business and have probably been to Las Vegas. The Mayor himself, wearing a navy pinstriped suit, and looking just well fed enough, told jokes to the same people. Ethel Merman, wearing a double-knit maroon dress with matching cape, was there. Carol Bellamy, the president of the City Council, wearing a blue silk shirt, a brown skirt, and a soubrette hairdo, was there. Estelle Parsons was there. A man who is a big television-film-property agent and who sometimes plays tennis with Jack Paar on weekends was there. Maureen Stapleton was there. E. G. Marshall was there. Celeste Holm was there. Shelley Bruce and Alice Ghostley, from the musical *Annie*, were there. Someone who looked just like Shirley MacLaine but wasn't Shirley MacLaine was there. When it was time to eat, the Mayor cupped his hands around his mouth and shouted "Come on down for lunch, everybody!" and at least three women in the room said "Oh, isn't he cute!"

After lunch (Scotch salmon, blanquette de veau with rice, carrots, pear tart), the mayor proposed a toast in which he said that New York was No. 1 again. Then he said that he had been on a radio show taking calls from listeners and one person had called in to complain about a two-hundred-and-fifty-pound naked woman cooking in a shopwindow. He said that he told the person calling in that he would have someone look into the matter officially. He said that he would now read from an official report he had received on the incident. He read, "Memorandum. To: Edward I. Koch, Mayor. From: Carl B. Weisbrod, Director, Midtown Enforcement Project. Re: Squat Theatre, West Twenty-third Street. We have investigated the complaint regarding a production at the Squat Theatre on Twenty-third Street during which a two-hundred-and-fifty-pound woman was reported to have performed nude in a storefront window. [Mild chuckle from guests.] It is true that this performance did indeed occur as described. It was, however, part of a radical avant-garde theatre group's play entitled *Andy Warhol's Last Love*. [Loud laughter from guests.]

The play itself was not written by Andy Warhol. [More loud laughter.] Nor did Warhol have any connection with this production, which has been described as the reflection of recent immigrant experiences in America. [Really loud laughter.] The production was staged by an extended family group of Jewish Hungarian refugees who fled from Hungary because they were about to be arrested for not conforming to the standards of Socialist Realism of the East Bloc nations. [Loud, loud laughter.] The play ended its run here in New York on September 15th. It is currently in production in Amsterdam, Holland, where the group will be spending the fall season. [Loud laughter.] The scene involving the naked fat woman in the window was part of this group's theory about 'inside' and 'outside' theatre. [More loud laughter.] They created a concept of performing before two audiences—the audience in the theatre and passersby on the street. The woman has been described as an authentic American witch who acts out a real witch's ceremony in the window. She was not cooking. [More loud laughter.] It is doubtful that her act would be declared legally obscene. [Mild laughter.] This play, supported with a grant from the New York State Council on the Arts [really loud laughter], was apparently very popular. It attracted an average of ninety per cent capacity audience. It received good reviews except from John Simon. [Loud laughter.] The theatre group, consisting of nine adults and five children, arrived in this country in June of 1977 under the aegis of the International Theatre Institute. It received an Obie for the play *Pigchild in Fire*, in 1977, and has been invited to represent the

United States at the Festival of Nations next spring in Hamburg, Germany. It is considered a serious group of artists who came to this country seeking freedom of expression through innovative methods. [Loud laughter and applause from guests.]"

—*November 20, 1978*

Recollections

✦

This hand-lettered invitation came in the mail. It read:

Mr. Alexander J. Burke, Jr.
President
McGraw-Hill Book Company
cordially invites

———   ———

to attend a luncheon
on Tuesday, the fourteenth of November
at half after twelve o'clock
in honour of
<u>ELVIS:</u>
<u>Based on the Recollections of</u>
<u>Lamar Fike and the American People</u>
by Albert Goldman

The Luncheon: Based on the recollections of some of the guests at the luncheon:

R. Couri Hay, celebrity columnist for the *National En-quirer* and star and producer of his own celebrity-interview show on Channel C, local cable-TV station: "The invitation was first-class. All the important media people were there. The narrated slide show of Elvis was outrageous. I just couldn't believe the dialogue. The lunch, I am sure, was very good. I couldn't stay. I had to get ready to leave for the Coast. And ever since I've been on TV I haven't been able to eat. I only wish I could have stayed, but I've got to rush off to the Coast."

Milton Glaser, illustrator and graphic designer: "We should get a rebate on the avocado crêpe with Louisiana cray-fish, but I thought the tournedos of beef was wonderful and the julienne autumn vegetables superb."

James McMullan, the illustrator: "It was very good, and I really appreciated the slides. This is my strongest impression of it: the focus wasn't on the book to come but on Elvis."

Anthony Delano, chief United States correspondent for the London *Daily Mirror*: "One has to be grateful for what it wasn't. It was not melon, dried-up filet mignon, sloppy pota-toes. They served a decent fourth-growth claret, and that alone was enough to distinguish it from a regular luncheon."

Alexander Burke, president of the McGraw-Hill Book Company: "It was a luncheon where we had a lot of fine peo-ple that we asked to come. I thought the people were better than the food."

A girl who wouldn't tell anything about herself: "Did you know that they've just *begun* to write the book? What if the author dies? Or Lamar Fike? Or the American people? Anyway, someone said that the book was to set the record straight, because Elvis Presley was a cultural institution and embodied the spirit of his age. Someone else said that Elvis Presley was an enigmatic personality. 'Enigmatic.' That's a word I hate completely."

—*November 27, 1978*

Off to China

R. Couri Hay, who is the celebrity columnist for the *National Enquirer* and the star and producer of his own celebrity-interview show on Channel C, a local cable-television station, said over the telephone the other day, "I am going to China. I will be there over the holidays. It's going to be very interesting, because, let's face it, China has turned around. My God, I think they are going to be welcoming us with American flags. I'm going with Zandra Rhodes. You know who Zandra Rhodes is? Well, she's in fashion. [We can't seem to escape it this week.] Zandra is taking her sketchbook, because they have promised to open up some museums for us. I'm sure her next collection will have a Chinese influence. I am taking summer clothes and winter clothes. I mean, we're going to hot China and cold China. I am taking jeans, of course, long underwear, L. L. Bean boots, my new Ralph Lauren baseball jacket lined with nutria. It's in red poplin. I'm not expecting any trouble in China. I mean, they are embracing capitalism. I am going to dress in red, white, and blue—I don't want peo-

ple to think I am Russian, or something. That should be fun.
I am hoping the hotels will be great. We're not allowed to tip,
but it was suggested to us that we take little trinkets. I am going to take key chains with the Empire State Building attached to them. That should be fun. We've also been told not
to take any ties or suits. Absolutely no ties. Interesting. For
me to go away on a vacation, I have to go to extremes to avoid
gossip. I mean, I can't just go to Europe, or something like
that. That's why I am going to China quick. With their new
capitalist thinking, and our recognizing them, and all that,
soon it might be like going to the Coast. I have been practic-
ing with my chopsticks, though secretly I am hoping the food
will be lousy, so that I can lose a few pounds. That's what I
would like while I'm there. A diet free of gossip and calories.
We're leaving from San Francisco and stopping off in Manila
to attend a dinner given by Mme. Marcos. Then to Hong
Kong, which is a pretty normal place. I think it's so interesting
how you get to places. We'll be going to China by train from
Hong Kong. That sounds interesting. When we get to China,
one of the places we are going to is Sian. Sian is such a mar-
vellous idea. I mean, this is so unseen by white eyes. Seven
months ago, I went to Cuba, but I had to go by way of Mex-
ico. When you go to these strange Communist countries, you
have to go to another country first. On the way back, I had to
charter a plane to the Bahamas. The pilot couldn't speak English. Later, I found out we almost crashed. He couldn't read
the map. But how many people charter a plane from Cuba?"

—*January 1, 1979*

Office Workers

✦⊱✧⊰✦

Our favorite highlights from *The Steelcase National Study of Office Environments: Do They Work?*, the published report of a survey conducted by Louis Harris & Associates, Inc.:

Eighty-two per cent of the office workers in this country have positive feelings about their jobs. There is little difference whether the person is male or female, or has been on the job more than six years or less than six years, and little difference whatever the type of job or the job level.

The three most important considerations that an office worker looks for in a job are clarity of the scope and responsibilities of the job, interesting work, and access to the tools, equipment, and materials needed to get the job done well.

During the past five years, seventy-three per cent of this country's office workers have had a change in the location of personal work space.

Ninety-four per cent of today's office workers feel that the way their personal work spaces look is important.

The two most important characteristics of a personal work space are how neat and well-organized it looks and the amount of privacy it affords. There is almost universal agreement on this among business executives and office workers.

More than seventy per cent of today's office workers are satisfied with their personal work spaces.

Office workers on the average spend only 6.4 hours per day at or in their personal work spaces.

The Harris people interviewed one thousand and forty-seven office workers, two hundred and nine executives, and two hundred and twenty-five office designers. None of the office workers, executives, or office designers mentioned the importance of nice, clear, long corridors or of Coke machines. A nice, clear, long corridor is an important thing to have in an office because office workers are then able to trip up or do a fireman's carry on an unsuspecting colleague. A Coke machine is important because an office worker can buy a nice, refreshing drink at it, stand around it and flirt, or sit on top of it stark naked while having a small nervous breakdown or while reading the poetry of Adrienne Barbeau.

—*January 8, 1979*

The World of Letters

Here is some information and advice that some editors of fiction (Thomas Congdon, editorial director of Thomas Congdon Books, E. P. Dutton; Thomas Dunne, executive editor, St. Martin's Press; George Glay, editorial manager, Harlequin Books; Newton A. Koltz, senior editor, Bantam Books; Richard Marek, president, Richard Marek Publishers; Maureen Baron, executive editor, Fawcett Books; Betty Prashker, editorial director of trade books, Doubleday; Ann Reit, editor, Scholastic Magazines; Sol Stein, novelist and publisher, Stein & Day) gave to some aspiring fiction writers, each paying twenty-five dollars (including lunch), at the Overseas Press Club the other day:

Word of mouth is what really sells a book. An ad in *The New York Times* doesn't necessarily help, but it's nice for the author.

Royalty statements are made out only every six months, because making them out costs a lot.

A fiction writer can write about anorexia nervosa, abortion, death, and homosexuality in hard-cover books for young adults but not in soft-cover books for young adults.

Teen-agers feel the same things as adults; they just don't have the words for them.

The teen-age book-publishing market is a flourishing book-publishing market.

Some fiction editors will buy a proposed book after seeing only a sample chapter and an outline. Sometimes an outline will be enough, sometimes a sample chapter will be enough.

Catch your reader in the first three pages.

Every chapter should make the reader want to go on to the next.

Chemistry is very important between writer and editor.

Big scenes are very important in a novel.

Deep editing is very important in putting a novel together.

Tremendous plot is not always important in writing a novel.

If you have been a nonfiction writer and want to be a fiction writer, that can be very frightening. Journalists are afraid of length; that may be why it is hard for them to write fiction.

—*February 12, 1979*

Over Here

A quick tour of the Antiques and Memorabilia Show at the Statler Hilton with the man in charge, Mort Berkowitz:

"Over here, we have some Joe Franklin sheet music. Do you know Joe? Joe was into nostalgia long before anybody else. Joe was here for two days. You just missed him. . . . Over here, everything from old shawls to umbrellas, including old plates. . . . Quilts here. . . . Porcelain to Chinese pots. . . . This is some old scrimshaw. Scrimshaw is engraving on bones or ivory—made popular on Nantucket in the time of Moby Dick. . . . And, of course, silver, which is always popular. . . . Antique jewelry. Sequins are pretty popular now that disco is in vogue. Any twenties or thirties fashions now that disco is in vogue. Did you know that this is the largest nostalgia show in the city? Nostalgia is very large. So many people long for the good old days, long for something meaningful. I mean, they long to regain their childhoods, don't you find? . . . You see those hats? Beautiful. . . . Of course, the Beatles are ever popular. And meet Helene, who is one of the largest Betty Boop collectors in the world. Hi, Helene. . . . This is really Art Deco. I don't know if you know Art Deco. Do you know Art Deco? . . . That's not an antique. That's just a little horse Kenny's mother gave him. You don't know Kenny. . . . A collection of tokens and coins. Richard, what were tokens used for, again?"

"Tokens were used as ads in giveaways to entice business and also to supplement the coins of the time."

"Thank you. That was very eloquent, Richard. What more can I say? . . . Over here, some books that we all read as children. . . . Oh, here is something interesting. Stuart, can you explain what this is?"

"This is a viewer for stereo cards and cabinet photos. The original piece, which looked just like this one, was invented in the eighteen-fifties by Antoine Claudet. Ten years later, the American manufacturers made the model that you are now looking at. Actually, this is a copy, in cherry wood. It is priced at three hundred and twenty-five dollars."

"Thank you, Stuart. Very good. . . . And, of course, there's Charles Lindbergh. He is ever popular. O.K.? O.K."

—*February 19, 1979*

Cat

❧❦❧

"News and Photo Tip:

"When: Monday, February 26th—11 A.M.

"Where: 1 Times Square, at 42nd Street (main floor).

"Why: The cat chosen for the role of Uncle Elizabeth in the forthcoming Broadway musical *I Remember Mama*, starring Liv Ullmann, will be introduced to the press. *I Remember Mama* will open on Broadway May 3, after its world-première engagement in Philadelphia March 9–April 21. Tara Kennedy, 7, who plays Miss Ullmann's youngest child in *I Remember Mama* and is the owner of Uncle Elizabeth in the musical, will be there to meet her stage pet. Tara comes from Scranton, Pa. She and the lucky feline will be making their Broadway débuts. Uncle Elizabeth's understudy will be introduced to the press at the same time."

Was the cat a big cat?

No. The cat was not a big cat. The cat was a very small cat.

Did you get very close to the cat? I mean, did you touch the cat?

No. I did not get too close to the cat. I mean, I am a little afraid of cats.

Did the cat have blue eyes?

No. The cat did not have blue eyes.

Did the cat look happy?

I wouldn't be able to tell a happy cat if I saw one. People say little babies don't smile. It's just their stomach griping. Someone said cats live the life of Riley.

Did the cat have a name?

Someone said that the cat's name was Jonesy.

Where did the cat come from?

Someone else said that originally she belonged to an actress but that the actress went to California to do television and couldn't take the cat.

Is the cat a light sleeper?

No. The cat is not a light sleeper. The cat is a regular cat sleeper.

Was the cat frisking about?

No. The cat was not frisking about. The cat was very passive.

Was the cat's coat beautiful?

No. The cat's coat was not beautiful. The cat's coat looked damp. It was raining that day.

Is the cat pretty?

No. The cat is not pretty. Not even for a regular house cat is the cat pretty.

What color is the cat?

The color of the cat is calico. From where I stood, not too close, the cat looked very dirty.

Did you fall in love with the cat all the same?

No. I did not fall in love with the cat all the same.

What does the cat like to eat?

I don't know, but she looked very thin.

—*March 12, 1979*

G-L-O-R-I-A

At a party that Doubleday (the publishers) gave for Gloria Vanderbilt, the author of a new book called *Woman to Woman*:

.... (*Sharp intake of breath*) "Gloria!"

.... "Gordon."

.... (*Sharp intake of breath*) "Gloria!"

.... "Ruth."

.... "Margaret."

.... "Tammy."

.... "Sean."

.... (*Sharp intake of breath*) "Gloria!"

.... "Remember when she dieted down to a hundred pounds?"

.... "Today, as you know, publishing is packaging."

.... "From where I stand, I can see a book titled *Beyond Defeat*."

.... "That is Gloria Jones."

. . . . "You mean . . . ?"

. . . . "Yes. There are an awful lot of famous Glorias here tonight. I am the least famous of them."

. . . . (*Sharp intake of breath*) "Gloria!"

. . . . "Jerry."

. . . . "Did Gloria design the suit and blouse she is wearing?"

. . . . "Gloria only designed the blouse."

. . . . (*Sharp intake of breath*) "Gloria!"

. . . . (*Sharp intake of breath*) "Gloria!"

Titles of some chapters or sections of Gloria Vanderbilt's book: "The Bright Garden of Memory—and Taste," "Early Me," "Learning More About Myself," "The Romance of the Self: Fortuny, Karinska, Adolfo," "Discovering Yourself," "The Spirit of the Artist," "Menus and Recipes."

There are many pictures in Gloria Vanderbilt's new book. Almost all of them have captions, and all of the captions perfectly describe the photographs: "Gloria in 1941." "Gloria in 1953—in a publicity photo for 'The Swan.'" "At sixteen Gloria on the brink of Hollywood." "Gloria dressed as a medieval damsel, Old Westbury, 1935." "The famous Sphinx photograph—Gloria wearing a Mainbocher gown." "Gloria in 1971—'the past few years have greatly expanded our sense of what we can be.'" "Gloria, with Carter Vanderbilt Cooper, wearing one of her Faraway coolie hats." "Gloria at work in her studio." "Gloria returns Wyatt Cooper's smile at a Broadway opening." "Gloria in the Ten Gracie Square days."

—*March 19, 1979*

The Ages of Woman

The Fragrance Foundation invited Dr. Susan Schiffman, Associate Professor, Department of Psychiatry, Duke Medical Center, to make an after-luncheon speech at the Plaza Hotel one day last month. Dr. Schiffman was asked by the Fragrance Foundation to try to explain to the guests, about two hundred perfume manufacturers and suppliers, an idea that the Fragrance Foundation had come up with, the idea being "The Five Fragrance Ages and Stages of Woman: Pre-Teen, Teen, Young Adult, Middle Age, Matron." From where we sat, this is some of what we heard Dr. Schiffman say:

"Thank you for a lovely introduction. Chemical senses are the most evolved . . . little bumps on your tongue . . . little oranges . . . emotional seat of the brain . . . a rat's brain . . . tongue . . . taste buds . . . olfactory receptors . . . turnover every ten days . . . moth-eaten by the time you get to be fifty-five . . . for some reason, turnover every thirty days . . . taste and smell acuity . . . taste buds . . . olfactory receptors . . . olfactory . . . hormones . . . taste and smell . . . depressed . . . a weight problem . . . mother and father saying territory to be established . . . I run a weight-loss unit . . . area of the brain . . . developing cigarettes for the Arabs . . . smell has something to do with territoriality . . . territoriality . . . of shame among young women . . . the first use of fragrance may be to define . . . very interested in female psychology . . . in the thirties, more comfortable . . . sexuality . . . emotional stimulant . . . sexual reason . . . overweight women . . . ten million receptor cells in the olfactory system . . . don't know what it is about musks that makes them, you know, so musky . . ."

—*April 9, 1979*

Festival

A press conference announcing a second Woodstock music festival. Some fragments from an exchange between the producers (whose backers include a record company and a film company) and the press:

"Ten years ago, a little magic happened that touched the nation, the world."

"I don't think we are fools."

"The reason that we want to do it is that since Woodstock there have been a lot of music films made and none of them had what 'Woodstock' had. The ten years since Woodstock have not been as exciting as the sixties."

"The tenth anniversary was a good time to do some of the things we hadn't been able to do last time. There is so much new technology today that you didn't have then."

"One word I would use to wrap up the whole thing is 'energy.' Try to turn that energy on."

"The kids, the youth . . ."

"No cultural event that sums up the seventies. This has

been a down decade, full of inflation, you know. No sense of optimism."

"Where will you hold this festival?"

"Even if I knew, I wouldn't tell you."

"We talked to the youngest, most exciting bureaucrats in this state. They believe in New York. They want us to stay here."

"How much money is going into it?"

"Money is coming from the record deal and the film deal."

"Six million dollars. Last time, we spent three million dollars. With inflation, everything is double."

"How much do you hope to get out of it?"

"Nobody is trying to get rich and retire from this."

"I've been involved in Indian projects for a while."

"Money. It's a real boring subject."

"Can you recapture the spontaneity?"

"Yes. No matter how much you plan, you can't kill spontaneity."

"We are not trying to kill the looseness of the event."

"What acts are you going to sign?"

"Can't say."

"You said you would never touch another rock festival. You said the first Woodstock was the worst disaster. Now . . ."

"No."

"It's an epochal festival."

"I could stand here until four o'clock and tell you what we are doing."

"What about drugs?"

"What *about* drugs?"

—*April 23, 1979*

Unveiling

❦

A number of sports personalities, sports-related personalities, and newsmen and newswomen from the papers and television, the mayor of New York City, the governor of New York State, Cardinal Cooke, and almost two hundred people who just happened to be passing by gathered the other day in the mall at Madison Square Garden to celebrate the hundredth anniversary of Madison Square Garden (there were three Madison Square Gardens before the present one, the first two really on Madison Square, and the third up at Fiftieth and Eighth) and to unveil a bronze statue of the goddess Diana, a duplicate of a statue of the goddess Diana which used to stand on top of the second Madison Square Garden.

Jack Dempsey was there, seated in a chair.

Dave Maloney, Phil Esposito, and Mike McEwen (the Rangers hockey stars) were there, and they stood behind Jack Dempsey, with their arms folded across their chests.

Joe Frazier was there, and he stood next to Jack Dempsey, with his hands folded across his chest.

A man wearing a toupee that made him look exactly like George Steinbrenner was there.

Jackie Stone, the television-news reporter, was there. After the taping of her report, she worried out loud about the angle at which her nose had been shot.

Howard Cosell, acting as master of ceremonies, was there.

Some of the people who were there made elaborate speeches. Some of the people who were there applauded the end of the elaborate speeches.

One man, whose name we didn't catch, named, in his elaborate speech, some boxing event as the most electric moment in the history of Madison Square Garden. Cardinal Cooke, in his elaborate speech, said that Madison Square Garden and St. Patrick's Cathedral were both a hundred years old this year. Howard Cosell began his elaborate speech, "I think you know the nature of the circumstances under which we are gathered here."

After that, Mayor Koch, Governor Carey, and a number of the other guests, grabbing the ends of two pieces of gold cord, unveiled the statue. The goddess Diana stood stark naked on tiptoe with a drawn bow.

—June 18, 1979

Miss Jamaica

❧❧❧

We met the current Miss Jamaica ("Joan McDonald, twenty-three years old, dance instructor at Wolmer's Girls' School, in Kingston; ardent supporter of dance and the cultural arts; has an interest in foreign languages; has two brothers and two sisters") at a cocktail party the other day. Miss Jamaica, like most beauty queens, seemed vivid and buoyant. Her nails were very long, and they were painted with a red lustre polish. She wore a beige shirtwaist dress with buttons down the front, but the dress was buttoned only to halfway down the skirt. She wore brown shoes with very high heels. When Miss Jamaica laughed—and she laughed a lot—she bent over and snapped her fingers. Also, when Miss Jamaica laughed we saw that she had big, white, almost perfect teeth.

At the cocktail party with Miss Jamaica and her guests were newsmen carrying small Japanese cassette recorders with huge microphones. They asked Miss Jamaica questions about the political aspects of being Miss Jamaica. This annoyed Miss Jamaica slightly, and she made some little sounds (sucking air in through the mouth with teeth clenched).

Miss Jamaica asked her chaperon for a cigarette. Then she said, "I was chosen from a field of twenty contestants in Kingston. I won the best-personality and best-photogenic categories. I am a member of the Jamaica School of Dance. I am a lover of the cultural and performing arts. When I was a child, I was very athletic—more athletic than anything else. I was pushed into—nicely pushed into—this contest. I was in my dance class one evening when one of the coördinators begged me, actually begged me, to enter the contest. I decided I had nothing to lose by entering. Right? Aha. As a matter of fact, I do think that anyone who feels she has the potential to be a beauty queen should try—*without* being pushed, like me. Not that I didn't have any confidence, but I didn't see myself as being a beauty queen."

"What is your favorite color, Miss Jamaica?"

"Color? I don't have a favorite color as such, but I do find that pastels look very good on me."

"What foods do you like to eat?"

"I like to eat a little bit of everything. As you can see, I don't have to watch my weight. I eat everything in the book."

"What are some of the places that being Miss Jamaica has taken you?"

"I have been to Germany. I was in the Miss World contest. I didn't place, but I understand I was very well liked. In London, I danced in bare feet just outside the House of Commons. This is my first visit here. New York is too crowded and fast-moving. Today, I had lunch at the World Trade Center. I got to see a view of Manhattan. I didn't like it. It's too ugly. Where are the mountains?"

—*July 2, 1979*

Hair

❧❦❧

News and Photo Tip:

When: Tuesday, June 26—10:30 A.M.

Where: The Plaza Hotel (59th and Fifth Ave.) Barber Shop, Mezzanine.

Why: Actor John Schuck (of TV's *McMillan and Wife*), who has a head of hair many men would die for, will have it all shaved off to play the shiny-domed Daddy Warbucks in the SRO Broadway hit *Annie* for three weeks (starting July 3) while the role's originator, Reid Shelton, enjoys a well-deserved vacation. Garren of the Plaza will do the shaving, and Shelton himself will be there to offer Schuck, who will be making his Broadway stage début, advice on the care of the Warbucks dome.

A woman said to John Schuck, "John, a lot of my bald friends would like to have your head of hair, and here you are shaving it off."

A man who was not bald said to John Schuck, "John, could you honestly say that bald men have more fun?"

John Schuck said, "Baldness brings a bit of authority. I think."

A man with a camera said to Reid Shelton, who was wearing a white suit, "That's a great suit, but isn't it hard to keep clean?"

Reid Shelton said, "I bought it for publicity. I was doing *The Merv Griffin Show* and I needed something with a little flash to it. But they are very hard to find—white suits."

John Schuck looked at the photographers jostling each other to get photographs of him and said, "The Normandy landings were nothing compared to this."

John Schuck's wife, Susan Bay-Schuck, who was standing nearby, looked at her husband's head, now half shaved, and grimaced. Then she reached out and touched it and said, "It feels pretty."

John Schuck said, "Why do I feel a draft?"

Reid Shelton said, "Oh, I'm glad John could come in. I need a vacation. I have been doing this for twenty-six months with only one time sick."

John Schuck felt his head, now completely shaved, and said, "It's the surface of the moon."

A man said, "Boy, I have seen better heads on cabbage," and everybody laughed.

Mrs. Schuck said, "Honey, it's not funny-looking at all."

Reid Shelton said, "Use a Norelco, I've told him. Use a Norelco."

Mrs. Schuck picked up some of her husband's hair from the floor and put it in a small brown envelope. She said, "If you get lonely, honey, you can open this and look inside."

—*July 9, 1979*

Thirty Years Ago

✦

A young woman we know writes:

Thirty years ago, Russia got the bomb; the Polaroid Land Camera was introduced, and sold for $89.75; the Methodist Church in the United States and Cuba had eight million six hundred and fifty-one thousand and sixty-two members; Tyrone Power married Linda Christian the day his divorce from a French film actress came through; Mickey Rooney married Martha Vickers the day his divorce from Betty Jane Rase came through; Lucille Ball remarried Desi Arnaz; Lady Astor said women should make the world safe for men; a survey found women in London too tired for social life; Dr. Benjamin Pasamanik was given the Lester N. Hofheimer Research Award (fifteen hundred dollars) for a study showing that Negroes had the same mental capacity as whites; Bill W., co-founder of Alcoholics Anonymous, told some psychiatrists that he had stopped drinking after accepting God; one of the five copies of the Gettysburg Address in Abraham Lincoln's own handwriting was sold to a Cuban at an auction for $54,000; Emperor Hirohito of Japan wrote a book about sea slugs, *An Illustrated Study of Opisthobranchiata in Sagami Bay*; a Gallup Poll found that the funniest American comedians were Bob Hope, Milton Berle, Jack Benny, Red Skelton, and Fibber McGee and Molly; the lost city of Peshawarun, Afghanistan, once used as a garrison by soldiers of Alexander the Great, was found; a broken plaster statuette of St. Anne, mother of the Virgin Mary, wept when Shirley Anne Martin, eleven years old, kissed it; Princess Margaret Rose of Great Britain and Northern Ireland was appointed head of the Girl Guides Sea Rangers; the Detroit Symphony cancelled its season because its musicians wouldn't take a cut in pay; Ruth Williams, an ex-stenographer from London, joined her new husband, Seretse Khama, Chief-designate of Bechuanaland's Samwangwato tribe; George Bernard Shaw said, "It is useless to go on ignoring the patent fact that Stalin is obviously the ablest statesman in Europe"; I was born.

That I was born thirty years ago doesn't seem to matter to anyone except my mother, my father, their families, and their friends. When I say to someone, "Thirty years ago, I was born," I can almost hear this running through their minds: "Yes. Yes. So you were born."

—*July 23, 1979*

Noon

✦

Where was everybody at noon on Monday, the tenth of September? At noon on Monday, the tenth of September:

We were at home, reading *The Little Sister*, by Raymond Chandler.

Don Clay, an interior designer, was sitting on a No. 3 Seventh Avenue subway train on his way to Wall Street. He had noticed, he later told us, that it was a beautiful day.

On the other hand, Edward Koch, the Mayor of New York City, was holding a meeting in his office. The subject under discussion was crime and public transportation. (The next day, the *News* carried a headline that read, "GARELIK FIRED AS TA COP BOSS.")

Moreover, Liz Smith, popular gossip columnist for the *News*, sat in her apartment—twenty-six floors up, with a spectacular view of the East River—finishing the next day's column. It was due at the paper at one o'clock, and the first paragraph read, " 'Sometimes I wonder if men and women really suit each other. Perhaps they should live next door and just visit now and then,' said Katharine Hepburn."

Enid Hunter, proprietress of Enid's, an antique-clothing store on Spring Street, stood in the doorway of her bedroom and looked around. "Today," she said to herself, "I will clean up and redecorate. I will hang some new pictures here and I will change around the chairs there. Today—that's what I will do today."

Brooke Norman accompanied her mother, Marsha Norman, to the hardware store to buy some tulip bulbs and to pick up some photographs of Brooke wearing her new one-shoulder bathing suit. She heard her mother say that she would try to force the tulips—red and yellow ones—to bloom indoors by Christmas. Then she accompanied her mother around the corner to the bank to deposit the church receipts from Sunday's service. Brooke Norman is almost two years old.

The attendant at the parking lot at Spring and Hudson Streets sat calmly in his shed. He looked out the window and waved to a woman passing, who did not wave back. A number of large trucks rolled by. Across the street, men went in and out of a topless bar that had a sign reading "Private. Members Only."

Vince Aletti, an A. & R. man for R.F.C./Warner Brothers Records, walked into the Strand Book Store. He went downstairs and stood in the section where they keep new books that are bought from book reviewers for a small fraction of the list price and offered to the general public at half the list price. Vince Aletti looked at the new half-priced books in stock. He looked at them for a long time, and then he said to himself, "The last thing in the world I need is another new book." He then walked out of the Strand Book Store. (Later, he couldn't remember if the sun had been shining or not.)

On the other hand, again, Reid Boates, the publicity manager for Doubleday & Company, was at a private luncheon in the company's private dining room. The private luncheon was held in honor of a woman who is writing a book about Ruth St. Denis. (Later, Reid Boates said "Let me see" when he was asked by a friend to give an account of the luncheon.)

A man walked into an auto-parts store and asked the salesman for a positive crankcase vent valve for his car and instructions for installing it. (Later, the salesman remembered that the customer had said he was taking a long trip and had heard that a positive crankcase vent valve would help with gas mileage.)

A young woman was lying on the shag-carpeted floor of a house on Canal Street. As she lay there, she closed her eyes and listened to an old song by Rick Nelson called "That's All She Wrote." When the record came to an end, the young woman got up and placed the needle back on the record so that she could hear the song over again. Then, opening her eyes before getting up the next time, she saw a large dark-gray mouse hopping and running only about three feet away from her. The mouse hopped because his little feet kept getting caught in the shag carpet. The young woman screamed loudly once; she screamed loudly again; she screamed loudly a third time. She later told us that no one, absolutely no one, heard her.

—*September 24, 1979*

Notes and Comment

A young woman we know writes:

This morning, I was listening to the radio—I mean, I was ironing my shirt and the radio was on—and the disc jockey said that the Beatles were getting back together, that they were going to give a benefit concert for some important cause or other, and how great that would be. He said, "Can you imagine the Beatles back and playing together?" I imagined that, and while I was at it I imagined a number of other things. I imagined that I was in love with the man who discovered the principle of hydrogen bonding and that he was in love with me, too, and that it was all almost wonderful; I imagined that my favorite color was red and that my favorite words were "vivid," "astonishing," "enigmatic," "ennui," and "ululating"; I imagined that even though I hadn't died I was in Heaven; I imagined that all the people I didn't like were gathered up in one big barrel and rolled down from a high mountain into a deep, deep part of the sea; I imagined that all the books on my shelf had long legs and wore flesh-colored panty hose and that their long legs in the flesh-colored panty hose dangled from the bookshelf; I imagined that the trains in the subway had all the comforts of a private DC-9; I imagined that I had the most beautiful face in the whole world and that some men would faint after they got a good, close look at it; I imagined that I had different-colored underwear for every day of the year; I imagined that it was a real pleasure to be with me, because I was so much fun and always knew the right thing to say when the right thing needed to be said; I imagined that I knew by heart all the poems of William Wordsworth; I imagined that it rained only at night, starting just before I fell asleep, so that the sound of the rain would lull me to sleep, and that it stopped raining just before I woke up every morning; I imagined that I could run my tongue across the windowpane and not pick up, perhaps, some deadly germ; I imagined that all the people in the world were colored and that they all liked it a whole lot, because they could wear outlandishly styled clothes in outlandish colors and not feel ridiculous; and then I again imagined the Beatles back and playing together. None of it did a thing for me.

—*November 19, 1979*

Mayor

One day recently, at about half past twelve, some people with disparate professional interests gathered at the site of the first City Hall in New York City, on Pearl Street—now a vacant lot—and waited for Mayor Koch, the city's Landmarks Preservation Commissioner, and an archeologist to say a few words about archeology, Old New York, immigrants, the Dutch, the city today, archeologists, the original shoreline of Manhattan, archeological digs in Jerusalem, archaeological roots in old Greece, and other things along those lines. The people were there at the request of the Landmarks Preservation Commissioner, a large man with large, very white teeth, which anyone could see when he smiled, and he smiled a lot. The Mayor was late, and these people whom the Landmarks Preservation Commissioner had invited to hear him, the archeologist, and the Mayor speak wandered around almost aimlessly when they weren't signing a piece of paper that said if they fell down and hurt themselves they wouldn't sue anybody. Then the Mayor arrived, and suddenly all these people, with their disparate professional interests, and maybe even disparate personal interests, found a common ground: all attention was now focussed on the Mayor. He walked over to the Landmarks Preservation Commissioner and the archeologist and greeted them. Then, while the Landmarks Preservation Commissioner and the archeologist made their speeches, the Mayor stuck his hands deep in his trouser pockets, glanced up and down, knit his eyebrows, made creases in his forehead, unmade the creases in his forehead, turned to look at what the people behind him were doing, looked up at the blue sky, looked down at his shiny black shoes, rubbed the area above his left cheek and just underneath his lower eyelid with the tip of his left index finger, put his left hand back in his left trouser pocket, pursed his lips, unpursed his lips, rocked his head from side to side, turned again to look at what the men behind him were doing, squinted his eyes, unsquinted his eyes, pressed his lips tightly together, then stretched them out in a Cheshire-cat smile, looked up at some pigeons flying by, took his left hand out of his left trouser pocket again, and rocked his head from side to side again. Later, we asked the Mayor what was going through his mind during the time the Landmarks Preservation Commissioner and the archaeologist were making their speeches. Without missing a beat, the Mayor said, "I was thinking how proud I am to be the one-hundred-and-fifth Mayor of the City of New York."

—*November 19, 1979*

Books

❧❦❧

Tammy Wynette, popular country-and-Western singing star, was in one of those large, supermarket-type bookstores on Fifth Avenue the other day autographing copies of her just published autobiography, called *Stand by Your Man*, which is also the title of one of her songs. She was sitting at a table, and in front of her on the table were stacks of the book. Tammy Wynette's husband, a man named George Richey, stood near the table. To one side of her were many people standing in a line and holding copies of the book, or record albums, or pieces of paper. Some of the people, when they got to her, said that they liked her jacket, which was purple. Some of the people, when they got to her, said that they liked her blouse, which was green. Other people said that they liked her jewelry—a gold chain worn around her neck and some rings on fingers of both hands. Still other people looked at her with smiles on their faces and said, "Your pictures don't do you justice." One man said to her, "You are absolutely gorgeous." She said to someone who asked her if she had just got into town, "Well, no. I did *Good Morning America*, I was on WHN, and I did the *Arlene Francis Show*." A man came up behind her and said, "You are the wildest woman in New York City," and she looked behind her and recognized the man and they hugged. She introduced him as a television interviewer from Nashville. She told a woman, who had asked, that her children listen to Elton John and Donna Summer. A woman told her that reading her book made her feel young again. Tammy Wynette shrugged and laughed. In the books she autographed, she wrote, alternately, "Thanks for asking. Love, Tammy" and "Hope you enjoy the book. Love, Tammy." Some of the people who asked her to autograph their books were named Don, Christian, Gillian, Paul, Bob, Dick, Paulette, Trixie, John, Regina, Lynn, and Mabel. Finally, she autographed a Xerox copy of a picture of herself standing near her swimming pool at her home in Florida, and autographed a copy of Lattimore's translation of the *Odyssey*, and then autographed some more books. After much prompting from her husband, she got into a car and was driven away.

—*December 3, 1979*

Colloquy About Sting

"Sting," said the pretty girl. "Sting. Sting. Sting. I just saw Sting and his band, The Police, play at the Palladium. They were great, but Sting was incredible. Sting is what I really like about the new rock and roll."

"Sting," said the man who was her companion. "Sting. I suppose I will be hearing a lot about Sting."

"Sting," said the pretty girl. "What did I really like most about Sting? It wasn't completely the way he held his bass guitar. It wasn't completely the way he wore his mechanic's jumper. It wasn't completely the fact that in his face he looks slightly savage. What did I like most about Sting?"

"Sting," said her companion. "Isn't it terrible what happened to him? He was walking down the street, minding his own business, when, suddenly, from out of nowhere, a large safe fell on his head."

"Sting," said the pretty girl. "Sting has such an unusual voice. Sting has such an interesting, unusual voice. Sting's voice is—well, mellifluous."

"Sting," said her companion. "How can I tell you this? Sting slept near an open window and he caught a terrible draft, and now every time he opens his mouth to sing, his poor throat just hurts and hurts, and he can't make a sound. Gosh, I'm really sorry."

"Sting," said the pretty girl. "Sting is in *Quadrophenia*. Sting was the best thing about *Quadrophenia*."

"Sting," said her companion. "Yes, Sting was the best thing about *Quadrophenia*. Too bad about that big truck bearing down on him so quickly as he crossed a busy intersection."

"Sting," said the pretty girl. "Sting. The way he danced. Very cool. It's a pleasure to see him move around."

"Sting," said her companion. "Sting. The way he *used* to dance. Too bad that now his feet aren't even attached to his body."

"Sting," said the pretty girl. "Sting has a very nice chest. When he came back onstage at the Palladium for his final encore, he had removed the top of his mechanic's jumper, so I could see his chest."

"Sting," said her companion. "Poor Sting. Did you hear what happened to him? He was chasing a stack of pancakes around a tree when he stubbed his toe on a tree root and hurt himself badly. Now he doesn't even have a chest."

"Sting," said the pretty girl. "Sting is the greatest person I have ever seen on a stage."

"Sting," said her companion. "Sting. Sting. Sting. Sting is greater than any living woman."

—*December 24, 1979*

Three Parties

"That man over there is a popular journalist," said a pretty girl. "He is at the center of things. He had an idea for an article, but then he saw his idea on *Prime Time Saturday*."

"I picked up a piece of cauliflower," said the man who was her companion. "I knew it was a piece of cauliflower. But just for conversation I said to a man standing next to me 'What is this?' and he said 'Oh, it's a *crudité*.' *Crudité*! Can you believe it? I mean to say, he was an American and he told me a piece of cauliflower was a *crudité*."

"That petite woman over there is a popular figure in modern dance," said the pretty girl. "She did the dance sequences in a very good movie, but the movie was a big flop. She is the only real artist in this room—she and the man over there who is playing the piano. He is a bad pianist playing bad show tunes. All men who play the piano are great artists."

"There's Bill Boggs," said her companion. "Bill Boggs is the only sane man in America. He is wearing a jacket with double vents. He is the only man in America who looks good in a jacket with double vents."

"That man over there is a famous producer," said the pretty girl. "I met him years ago. He took out a girl I knew then. He made love to her in the shower."

"Right next door is another party," said her companion. "A dinner party. People from a paper company. Perhaps they are very happy and will soon be eager to show it."

"I have just remembered something," said the pretty girl. "I once stood in this very room and a woman showed me twelve different ways to wear the same dress. She was from Japan. It wasn't a very interesting idea."

"Blythe Danner is standing over there talking to someone who could be a jerk or who could be Francis of Assisi," said her companion. "I have no real thoughts on Blythe Danner."

"That woman in the red cowboy boots once wrote a long article about Stevie Wonder," said the pretty girl. "I admire all women, even when they haven't discovered something as important as radium."

"There is a reporter here from *People* magazine," said her companion. "The same man, who lives in Greenwich Village, makes out our taxes."

"All the people in this room care very much for each other," said the pretty girl. "Look at how interested each one is in what the others are saying. I am sure they call each other up every day just to make sure that not one of them is running a fever."

"Those two people are from Italy," said her companion.

"They don't know who the man is they are talking to. Slowly, and using on-the-spot sign language, he is telling them."

"Unknown to me, someone took my picture," said the pretty girl. "I can feel myself losing altitude. I can feel my halo evaporating in the clear winter air. I can feel my spirit taking a long walk away from me."

"There's nothing out there," said the pretty girl's companion. "There's nothing out there except sometimes you see big rats—the kind that come from Norway. Or people in bootleg-cut jeans."

"Rats have buck teeth," said the pretty girl. "That is, they do unless they gnaw on something."

"When I look at Rockefeller Center," said her companion, "I say to myself, 'Now, that's a tribute to something.'"

"I knew a man who used to take three teaspoons of sugar every day in his morning coffee," said the pretty girl. "Three teaspoons of sugar. While he was drinking it, he said, he felt like Atlas. But shortly after, he said, he felt as sluggish as a mole."

"Fifth Avenue and Forty-ninth Street," said her companion. "I ran into a woman I used to know, and she had just spent the summer in Montana. She said, 'This summer and fall in Montana, four hundred and fifty-six thousand six hundred and twenty-three dozen eggs, two hundred and eighty thousand six hundred and twenty-nine chickens, and forty-eight hundred pigs were destroyed because the feed had become contaminated with a chemical that causes cancer in animals.' I didn't tell her that that was not news to me."

"Talk about sugar!" said the pretty girl. "I heard of a man who lived in Harlem and for breakfast he ate Hostess Twinkies and cola soda. Every day, he ate that, and every day he went out and committed a gruesome crime. When he was finally caught, he pleaded sugar rush."

"When I look at the Empire State Building," said her companion, "I say to myself, 'Now, that's another tribute, to an entirely different thing.' When I look at the Empire State Building, I make a mental note of all the things I really need."

"I took a trip to Port of Spain once," said the pretty girl. "On a banana boat. I ate a lot of bananas, I was bitten by a lot of fleas, and a man who drank rum talked in my face constantly. For a long time afterward, it was no to bananas, fleas, and men."

"The people here," said the pretty girl, "don't like to dance to the new Joe Jackson record, or the new Police, or the new Talking Heads, or the new Tom Petty, or the new Clash, and they don't know how to dance to ska music. All the people here are older young white people. They like to dance to any Motown record from 1965."

"Well, well," said her companion. "Well, well."

"Last night, I dreamed that I was at a party with all these people," said the pretty girl. "The party was on the thirty-second floor. I willed all the guests to go out on the balcony, hold their nose, and jump."

"Well, well," said her companion.

"I danced with that woman in the man's suit," said the pretty girl. "As I danced with her, I knew she was a woman in a man's suit. And I danced with her as if she were a woman in a man's suit. When the dance was over, she said, 'I bet you didn't know that I was a woman wearing a man's suit.' I didn't say anything, but I thought, I bet you don't know that a potato when cooked has only about a hundred and twenty-five calories."

"Well, well," said her companion.

"This is my last party," said the pretty girl. "Tonight, as I was getting dressed, I said to myself, 'This is my last party.' On a cold night like tonight, I wear long underwear. Leaf-green-color long underwear. I said to myself as I was putting on my long underwear, 'This is my last party.' "

"Well, well," said her companion.

"The next time I get an invitation to a party," said the pretty girl, "I will say to myself, 'All those fish heads I have in the freezer—it's time to make a soup out of them.' "

"Well, well," said her companion.

—*January 14, 1980*

Expense Account

❦

Expense account for press breakfast for Milton and Rose Friedman, the Nobel Laureate economist and his wife, in honor of their new book and PBS television series, *Free to Choose: A Personal Statement*:

(1) Cost of transportation to and from press breakfast for this reporter (by subway) $1.00

(2) Cost of clothes this reporter wore to press breakfast, including makeup and hairpins (wild guess) $65.00

(3) Cost of building in which press breakfast was held $40,000,000.00

(4) Cost of transportation to and fro for other reporters (off-the-top-of-the-head guess, making allowance for the fact that some of them may have taken cabs, or the train from Connecticut) $250.00

(5) Cost of clothes other reporters wore to press breakfast . . . .(too complicated to make even a wild guess)

(6) Cost of heating pressroom for a couple of hours (another wild guess) $10.00

(7) Cost of Milton Friedman's well-pressed suit . . .$250.00

(8) Cost of Milton Friedman's shiny black made-in-Hong Kong shoes $20.00

(9) Cost of Milton Friedman's tie (with a pattern of Adam Smith portraits) $10.00

(10) Cost of Milton Friedman's neat haircut $5.00

(11) Cost of Rose Friedman's royal-blue Ultrasuede suit $300.00

(12) Cost of Rose Friedman's blue polyester blouse . .$35.00

(13) Cost of Rose Friedman's black mid-calf-length boots $50.00

(14) Cost of Rose Friedman's brown Mark Cross handbag $100.00

(15) Cost of breakfast (including coffee, cream, sugar, 6-oz.-can servings of orange juice, fruit cup, bagels and bialys, smoked salmon, cream cheese, tea, and two people to serve the guests) $420.00

(16) Cost of press kits (including one or two free books given to press people) $500.00

(17) Cost of phone calls made by press people from the press breakfast to the office $1.75

(18) Cost of ball-point pen held by reporter who looked like the actor who played Dr. No in the movie *Dr. No* . . . .$.59

Total $40,002,018.34

—*January* 20, 1980

The Governor's Party

NEWS RELEASE:

GOVERNOR'S OFFICE FOR MOTION PICTURE AND
TELEVISION DEVELOPMENT IN NEW YORK, CRE-
ATED TO ATTRACT FILMMAKERS TO THE STATE,
HOSTS LUNCHEON TO CALL ATTENTION TO
RECORD AMOUNT OF FILMMAKING CURRENTLY IN
NEW YORK.

There were twelve photographers; there was Sylvester Stallone, wearing an ill-fitting double-vented suit; there was the former Miss India, one of the stars of *Star Trek—The Motion Picture*, in which she appears completely bald; there was Billy Dee Williams, with his hair lying flat on his head, as if it had just been pressed; there was a man named Martin Poll, a producer, who has a wife named Gladys; there was a man who could have been a fishing-equipment salesman, because he looked so much like a smart old trout; there was an editor from *Us*; there was the woman who writes the "Newsmakers" page for *Newsweek*, and she had a lot of nice things to say about a stunning blond protégée of Mickey Rooney and a lot of not too nice things to say about the people she worked for, who weren't going for a picture layout with a mention of the stunning blond protégée of Mickey Rooney; there was a man who said, "Isn't Martin bold? He's producing in Italian and shooting in New York"; there was a woman who had just won an emerging-artist grant from the National Endowment for the Arts for her photographs of people at parties; there were quite a few bowls filled with ground raw red meat; there was a woman who had known for twelve years a man who has written a book on De Quincey and a book on Lenny Bruce; there was a man who said quite matter-of-factly that he had been a member of the United States Army Special Forces; there was a woman who left her handbag under a table and then, when someone moved the table, couldn't find her handbag; there was a woman who said, "See *Being There*. It is an American movie with an arty European feel to it"; there was a woman who didn't want her picture taken with Sylvester Stallone—the only woman who didn't—and who wondered out loud just what Sylvester Stallone, the former Miss India, and Billy Dee Williams were saying to each other for the full forty-five minutes that they stood around in front of the twelve photographers having their picture taken; then there was Earl Wilson, speaking to Sylvester Stallone, and all the time jotting down in a small brown notebook things Sylvester Stallone told him. A couple of days later, in his column, Earl Wilson wrote:

Sly Stallone was wearing a very dark beard. He looked like a great blackberry pie with a face in the middle. Slickly neat in a grey suit, he moved about quickly, authoritatively, at Maxwell's Plum. The Governor's Office for Motion Picture Development was giving a party for Martin Poll's new film *Attack*, with Sly as a decoy cop.

"Welcome back to New York," I said. . . . "Thank you, I'm looking for a new home, I may move back—if they'll have me. I'll be here 13 weeks. We'll see how it feels."

I was keeping some pretty female journalists from gasping over him. He was busy but polite.

—February 18, 1980

Sara

❧❧❧

Command: Find a new Little Miss Marker.

Question: Who is the new Little Miss Marker?

Answer: The new Little Miss Marker is a little girl who is six years old. Her name is Sara Stimson, and she is from Helotes, Texas. She has dark hair and dark eyes, and she has a line of little girls' clothes named after her, a doll that looks more or less like her named after her, and a fruit punch for anybody who wants to drink it also named after her. Her mother, who goes with Sara wherever Sara goes, carries in her pocketbook a can of Band-Aids, a small bottle of Mercurochrome, a jar of baby aspirin, a tube of medicated ointment, and packets of Baby Fresh towellettes. Sara's mother's name is Dana. Dana says, "We are from near San Antone, Texas. I was working as a secretary at the V.A. hospital when a friend of mine came in and said they were interviewing little girls for a movie—a modern remake of the old Shirley Temple movie *Little Miss Marker*. You know, if you have kids, you like to expose them and you want to see if they have a talent for something. I told Sara to get dressed and comb her hair, and I would take her and see if she wanted to talk to these people. Well, when she got there, she just chatted with them and really opened up. They videotaped her and sent the tape to Universal Studios. Universal liked it and asked us to come for a screen test. It will be a year ago tomorrow that we went out to Hollywood. When they asked us to come out, I thought it would be an adventure for Sara. She had never flown before. Now she has flown a bunch. There were eight little girls tested that day. We went back home and waited, and then they called us one Tuesday and asked us to come back on a Sunday. Of course, you lie in bed and you say, 'What is this going to be? Are you going to end up with a Judy Garland or a Marilyn Monroe?' I would like to see Sara have a normal life. That's what's important to me. The money? I don't care about the money. It took them three months to make the movie. Now comes the big publicity. She has done Dinah Shore, Merv Griffin, Mike Douglas. She is an extremely bright little girl. She has good manners, and she is very unselfish. She is just the furthest thing from self-centered that you can find. She cleans up around the house, makes her bed, plays with the neighbors. She likes applesauce, chocolate ice cream, Twinkies, bubble gum, *I Love Lucy*. She goes to public school and is in the second grade. She's never had an acting lesson, and she has no problems learning her lines. On the set, she liked everybody. It's as if God said, 'Where can we find a kid who will be just great to play Little Miss Marker?' "

—*March 17, 1980*

Runner

We saw a beautiful nine-year-old girl named Machelle Sweeting win the Colgate Women's Games VI eight-hundred-metre run, at Madison Square Garden. She ran so fast and she ran so gracefully that at times she seemed to be not a little girl running in an arena but a young, long-limbed animal running on the veldt. The other day, we went up to Harlem and called on Machelle Sweeting. With her in her family's living room were her mother, Mary; her father, Eddie; her sister, Elizabeth; her brother, Glenn; and her seventeen-year-old track coach, Kevin Moore. Machelle at first appeared shy, so her mother, a handsome and expansive woman, said, "Machelle has won around thirty races in the last year and a half. She has only been running for two years, and competing for less than that. I cannot believe it. She was born with a dislocated hip, and the doctors thought that she would never be able to walk at all. I discovered her dislocated hip when she was three months, and when I took her to the doctor they wanted her to have an operation. I said no, she was too young. They designed a special brace for her, and she wore it until she was thirteen months. She started to run because her sister Elizabeth was running. I didn't want her to run—I was always afraid she would do something to her leg. But Kevin, who was also Elizabeth's coach, kept encouraging her. In a year and a half, she has won fifteen first-place trophies, one for third place, and one for fourth. She is part of a relay team that is No. 1 in the country for girls nine years and under. That one over there is my favorite of all her trophies—the East Coast Invitational. She broke the national record on her first day, and on the second day she broke her own record. She is a very bright girl. She has won a Kiwanis Science Award for an electricity project. She painted a shoebox blue, put a light bulb in the top, connected two wires to a battery and the light bulb, and made the box light up. She writes poetry and has won a special award from the World Poets' Resource Center—it does a lot locally to promote student poetry. She is in the third grade, and is her class president and an honor student. For one of her class projects, she wrote a book called *How the Zebra Got His Stripes*. Her reading score is 6–9."

By then, Machelle wasn't feeling so shy.

We asked her what she liked to do besides running.

She said, "I like to sing television commercials and I like to mimic my mother." She proceeded to sing a television commercial for the Broadway show *Peter Pan* and one for the Broadway show *Evita*, and she sang the song in the Trident sugarless-gum commercial and the song in the commercial for Sasson jeans. Then she mimicked the voice of her mother, just home from her job at an Off-Track Betting office and tired, on the telephone with a friend. Then she said to us, "I like spinach, I like carrots, I like peas and rice, I like steak, I like celery, I like ice cream, I like chocolate, and I like to paint—especially with the color blue."

—*March 31, 1980*

Party

"Well, here we are at a party celebrating the fiftieth anniversary of the publication of the first of the Nancy Drew mystery books!" exclaimed Pam.

"Yes, here we are," said her friend Bess, with a short toss of the head.

"Yes, here we are," echoed Sue, Bess's younger sister, and then, with a challenging look at her two companions, "So now what?"

"Some stairs," said Pam, pointing and then leading the way. "Let's take these stairs."

"Oh, oh, oh," groaned Bess as she slowly followed Pam up the steep marble stairs. "Instead of stairs, I want some refreshments immediately."

"Do I have to come with you?" asked Sue, with a touch of the querulous little sister in her voice.

"I like looking down from the tops of stairs at people who are just milling about," said Pam, ignoring her companions and dashing up the stairs two at a time. Then, reaching the landing, she turned and looked down on a room filled with people who were in fact milling about and who also held glasses in their hands.

"Refreshments," said Bess, licking her lips thirstily. "I wonder where those people got their refreshments."

"Shall I go all the way down and ask them for you?" asked Sue, with more than a little sarcasm. "And then shall I come all the way back up and give you the information?"

Suddenly, Pam's body tensed; her fingers grew taut as she clutched at the balcony rail. "Look!" she exclaimed in a soft but hoarse whisper. "Look," she said again, and this time she pointed a finger at something or someone down below.

"Oh, oh, oh," said Bess, her eyes growing large and her face turning first a ghostly white, then a vivid red.

"What?" asked Sue, peering at the swirling mass, her head bobbing up and down confusedly.

"But it can't be," said Pam.

"I don't believe it," said Bess.

"What?" asked Sue again, this time with a small stamp of the foot.

"How vile!" said Pam.

"How vile, to say the least!" said Bess.

". . . But . . ." said Sue.

"How bilious!" said Pam.

"How bilious indeed!" said Bess.

"I . . . I . . . I . . . don't know . . . what you are talking about," said Sue, with an almost prehistoric whine in her voice.

"Shall we?" asked Pam, turning to Bess and grabbing her almost roughly by the shoulders.

"Shall we? Shall we?" said Bess, trying to free herself from Pam's now firm grasp.

"Hypers," said Sue. "Shall we what?"

Pam, now locked in indecision, turned back to whatever it was that had caught her attention so firmly before. Her face darkened in puzzlement, her eyes darting here and there furiously and fast. "It's gone," she said. "Oh, dear! It's gone."

"It's gone," said Bess. "It is gone. Oh, oh, oh."

"But what?" said Sue. "And now it's gone. And now I don't suppose you will ever tell me. You never tell me anything."

—May 12, 1980

Royalty

❦

The other morning, Their Royal Highnesses Prince Albert and Princess Paola of Belgium, here to celebrate the one-hundred-and-fiftieth anniversary of the independence of Belgium, were expected at a quarter past nine in the lower plaza of the McGraw-Hill Building to see *The New York Experience*, a film about how truly awful but truly wonderful it is to live in New York. At twenty-five minutes past nine, Their Royal Highnesses Prince Albert and Princess Paola had not arrived, and the publicity man for Trans-Lux, owners and operators of the film, was beginning to get nervous, because the film ran for a full hour, and at eleven o'clock three hundred school-children were scheduled to see the show. Standing alone at the foot of the escalator, looking up quickly every time he heard footsteps approaching, he said, "If they are really late, I don't know what we are going to do." He also said, "Ah, the vicissitudes of publicity. The TV people were to be here, but they're stuck in New Jersey. They had it on their books. I was on the phone with them this morning. But now they're in

New Jersey." And he said, "I hear that the Prince and the Princess are staying at the Waldorf, and that the city didn't even give them a police escort around town. Can you imagine? Royalty and no police escort!"

At half past nine, the publicity man looked up and saw twenty men, each wearing a dark suit, each with a little red-and-white card indicating that he represented the Belgian press, come down the escalator, and the publicity man sighed and shook his head. In the next fifteen minutes, a woman carrying a large shopping bag, a man wearing a golfing shirt, two women chatting in French, and a man wearing a pin-striped suit with a woman wearing a blue dress came down the escalator, and each time the publicity man sighed and shook his head. Then, at a quarter to ten, he looked up and saw a man followed by a large group of people come down the escalator. He said, "This must be the Prince." And it was.

The publicity man held out his hand, tipped forward slightly, and said to the Prince, "Welcome, Your Highness."

The Prince and the publicity man shook hands, and then the Prince started to move on.

"Where is the Princess?" asked the publicity man.

"Alas," said the Prince, "the Princess could not come."

"Oh," said the publicity man. "I am sorry." His face fell a tiny, tiny bit. But then, catching himself, he said, "Well, if you'll just come over here, I would like to have a picture of you standing in front of this poster." The poster advertised *The New York Experience*.

—*June 2, 1980*

Two Book Parties

❧❧❧

ONE: The *Balletomania: A Quizzical Potpourri of Ballet Facts, Stars, Trivia, and Lore*, by Andrew Mark Wentink, party:

1. Who wore combs in her hair at this party?
   a. Patricia McBride.
   b. Mme. Marie Taglioni.
   c. Birgit Cullberg.
   d. The Duchess of L'an L'ing.
   e. Marie Merchant.
2. Where was this party held?
   a. At a friend's house.
   b. On the roof of a building.
   c. In a private supper club.
   d. At the Vincent Astor Gallery
      in the library at Lincoln Center.
   e. I give up.

3. At this party there was one woman who

    a. said in a loud voice, "This is Ruth Page."

    b. blew kisses across the room to women she obviously didn't even know.

    c. had a huge pile of dry wood on her head.

4. At this party, there was a man in a khaki-colored suit, and his name was

    a. Peter Marshall.

    b. James Van Allen.

    c. Anthony Dowell.

    d. Harvey Fuqua.

    e. Álvar Núñez Cabeza de Vaca.

5. At this party, there were a lot of

    a. things to drink.

    b. races to run.

    c. closets to clean.

    d. babies to feed on time.

6. At this party, one girl said,

    a. "I want to live now."

    b. "*Close Encounters* was a movie, *1941* was a film."

    c. "I have never in my entire life seen anything like it."

    d. "I think being funny is a joke."

    e. "I want to go home now."

7. At this party, people were

    a. talking animatedly to each other.

    b. reading the *Introduction to the Principles of Morals and Legislation*, by Jeremy Bentham.

    c. looking at decorator colors on a paint chart.

8. At this party, a different girl from the one mentioned earlier said,

    a. "Boy, if I never go to another book party I wouldn't care. This is the best book party I have ever been to."

    b. "I like hot dogs."

    c. "It's just amazing how good I can be when I put my mind to it."

    d. "Yes, I know what you mean."

    e. "I want to go home now."

Answers: 1, a; 2, d; 3, a; 4, c; 5, a; 6, a; 7, a; 8, e.

Two: The *Baseball Diamonds*, edited by Richard Grossinger and Kevin Kerrane, party:

The man from one of the city's daily newspapers walked up to the bar and asked for a drink. He had to ask for it a couple of times before anyone seemed to even notice he was there. When he finally got his drink, he drank it. In one gulp. The drink obviously went down his throat straight to the bottom of his stomach, and stayed there—at least for a little while. The man from one of the city's daily newspapers asked for another drink, and after he drank that one he asked for another, and after he drank that one he asked for another. This was one for his stroll around the room. As he strolled around the room, he greeted people, some of whom he knew—they were in the daily-newspaper business—and some of whom he was meeting for the first time. Clearly, he was glad to be in this room, glad to be with these people, glad to have a drink in his hand, glad to be alive. A woman came up to him and said, "Hi, I like your great writing," and the combination of the drinks and the woman's saying such a thing to him made his face turn red with pleasure. He beamed at her, and she, in turn, beamed at him. As he moved on, he shook his head and shaped his eyes into a playful squint. The words "Well, well" formed on his lips, and he put his free hand on his nape, perhaps reminding himself that he was, after all, a man from one of the city's dailies. He said out loud to himself, "I better call my wife." His clear blue eyes suddenly clouded over. He said, "I better get out of here." He looked up. His eyes met those of another woman. She wore a black dress, a white apron, and a little white cap. She was one of the waitresses hired specially for this party. He looked at her, his eyes pleading. She looked back at him, and in looking so closely and deeply at him she knew everything about him there was to know at that moment. She brought him a fresh drink.

—June 23, 1980

Audition

❧✦❧

Lester Lanin, the society bandleader, who is from Philadelphia, who as a child played the piano and the drums, who has played at more than ten thousand weddings and at more than three thousand débutante parties, who has played in every state of the union except Montana, who has committed to memory the tunes of many thousands of songs, who is in his sixties, who has been conducting a Lester Lanin Orchestra since 1937, who was once married to a woman who was a former Miss Texas, held an open audition recently in a room he rented for four hours in a building on Broadway. Sixty-three musicians showed up for the audition. They had heard about it either from the musicians'-union paper or from a column in the *Post* or by word of mouth. Of the sixty-three musicians who showed up, five were women, one of whom played the flute, one the trumpet, one the harp, and the two others—sisters, who had just come from playing on the *QE2* eighty-day 1980 World Cruise—the violin and the accordion.

It was raining heavily on the day Lester Lanin held the audition, and almost everybody in the studio—a large, white, square room with mirrors covering one wall—looked a little rumpled and damp, the way people look when they have just come in out of the rain. Lester Lanin did not look rumpled and damp. He wore a neatly tailored black suit with a vest, a black-and-white patterned shirt, and a black-and-white patterned tie. He is a small man, about five feet seven, and he stood more or less in the center of the room, surrounded by auditioning musicians—say, a pianist, a drummer, a bass player, a clarinettist, a trumpet player, a trombonist, a flutist, and a guitarist. Every fifteen minutes or so, a new group of musicians assembled. Each musician was asked to play something, and the others joined in.

"Do you know ' 'Swonderful'?" Lester Lanin asked a man who played the trumpet.

"Yes," said the man. He started playing " 'Swonderful," and the other musicians did their best to join him.

"That's good," said Lester Lanin. "But a couple of notes were a little corny. Try 'Somebody Loves Me.' "

Altogether, in a period of four hours, Lester Lanin asked thirty musicians to play "Somebody Loves Me," thirty musicians to play "All the Things You Are," thirty-five musicians to play " 'Swonderful," twenty-seven musicians to play "Willow Weep for Me," forty-two musicians to play "Muskrat Ramble," one musician to play "Proud Mary," three musicians to play "Bad Girl," the same three musicians to play "Hot Stuff," four musicians to play "Macho Man," one musician to play "Freak

Out," ten musicians to play "Hello, Dolly!," one musician to play "Ease On Down the Road," two musicians to play "Just the Way You Are," and one musician to play "Moonlight Becomes You." When any of the musicians didn't know the tunes to the songs, Lester Lanin told them to go out and buy a certain songbook, which had over five hundred songs in it, and learn all the songs in the book. He told them that in his orchestras, of which he sometimes had as many as forty, no one played from sheet music—only from memory. To a man who was a very good trombone player but knew only one of the tunes he was asked to play, Lester Lanin said, "Many famous orchestra musicians have played with me, but they weren't qualified to play a deb party or other social event, because they couldn't play the tunes without charts."

At the end of the audition, Lester Lanin said he thought he would use men who had played the clarinet, the flute, the guitar, and the trombone, and the two sisters who had just come off the QE2 tour.

—*August 4, 1980*

Benefit

Gary Indiana, the punk poet and pillar of lower-Manhattan society, said:

Last night, I m.c.'d a benefit for myself at the Mudd Club, on White Street. A couple of weeks ago, someone broke into my apartment and took the money I had to pay the rent, and my videotape machine and my stereo, which weren't even really mine. I felt like a refugee, and so I gave myself a benefit. Tina L'hotsky showed three films—*Marilyn*, *Snakewoman*, and *Barbie*. Then Ethyl Eichelberger, along with John Heys and Agosto Machado, did some music from their play, which is a new version of *Medea*. They did a number called "Revenge." Ethyl, of course, is this drag performer wearing Kabuki eye makeup. Then Max Blagg came on and read some of his poems. I don't know if you know Max. Max is this decadent Englishman. He writes poems about his own feckless romanticism. He is always falling in and out of love. His poems are in the form of letters sent from hotels in South America.

People loved it. They wanted more. So Max, backed up this time by Ethyl, came back, and he read while Ethyl played. That was pretty good. Rene Ricard read a poem called "Prison." Rene is in *Underground USA*. It's the cult film of the year. Rene also had a small part in *The Chelsea Girls*, and he was in another film, called *Hall of Mirrors*, which Warren Sonbert made in 1966. Around that time, when he was twenty, Rene was probably the most good-looking man in all of New York. Gerard Malanga read some of his poems. One had something in it about some kids at Bennington, and people didn't like it very much. I mean, this crowd didn't care about Bennington. Then Cookie Mueller read a long story about living in San Francisco. It was about all the things she did, and it was fabulous. People loved that. I think they liked that best of all. Cookie is in all the John Waters movies, and a lot of people know her from that, but I don't think many people knew that she wrote. I read my new poem, which is almost entirely based on "You've Really Gotta Hold on Me" and "You're the Top." A lot of people I didn't even know showed up, but I recognized James Rosenquist, Michel Auder, Chi Chi Valenti, Patti Astor, Kathy Ruskin, and Richard Sohl. I came out of it with four hundred dollars, and I am going to buy a new lock for my door and go to the dentist.

—*September 8, 1980*

New

At a luncheon, at the Regency Hotel, in honor of Cyd Charisse, the dancer and actress, because her legs were the first pair of legs to be elected to the newly established publicity abstraction called the Hall of Fame for Famous Legs, two women said these things to each other:

FIRST WOMAN: Men don't know how to talk to each other. Men will go out and they will play a game of tennis and they will have a drink, but they don't know how to touch. They don't know how to get into their emotions.

SECOND WOMAN: Yes.

FIRST WOMAN: I feel sorry for men. I look at them and they look so helpless, and I think, God!

SECOND WOMAN: Yes.

FIRST WOMAN: I think things are changing little by little, though. I think among a few men there is beginning to be some loosening up.

SECOND WOMAN: Yes.

FIRST WOMAN: I was talking to the designer Emanuel Ungaro the other day, and I asked him, because he is a Frenchman, who of the men he knew in America today he would say represented this new kind of attitude in American men. I mean men who are beginning to seem more open about themselves, about the problems men have getting through in the world, about how they really deal with their feelings. And you know what he said? He said that the only man he could think of was Alan Alda. And you know what? I had to agree with him.

SECOND WOMAN: Yes.

FIRST WOMAN: Alan Alda is a very interesting man. Did you know he was named Man of the Year? I have heard him talk on television shows about his life. He is very sensitive to the needs of women—especially women in a marriage situation. You know, he is the star of a TV show and he has to work in Hollywood, but he makes sure that every weekend he gets home to New Jersey and sees his wife and his children, and he and his wife talk to each other every day. And I don't know if you know that he is a very good-looking man. But that's it— he doesn't let his good looks go to his head. He's still regular, he still wants to go home to his wife, he still wants to see his children. I think that will be part of being the new type of man we'll be seeing. I think that men will know that they are good-looking and they will just go beyond it, you know—not try to use it like some kind of weapon. Then they can get into other areas, other things.

SECOND WOMAN: Yes.

FIRST WOMAN: Are you married?

SECOND WOMAN: Yes.

FIRST WOMAN: Then you know what I am talking about?

SECOND WOMAN: No.

—*October 6, 1980*

Great

Merv Griffin, that great bon-vivant television-talk-show host extraordinaire, has written his autobiography, and to celebrate its publication Richard E. Snyder, the president of Simon & Schuster (and the publisher of Merv's book) threw a party for Merv Griffin in his penthouse suite at the St. Moritz Hotel. Almost everything about this party was great: the food (platters of cold cuts, cheese, pâté, bowls of black olives, three different kinds of bread) was great, and there was lots of it; the flowers were great, and they were all over the place and they were real; the chess set that was there just in case anyone wanted to play a game of chess was great, and it had a real marble board; Bobby Short, the great saloon singer and pianist, was there, and he looked great; Edwin Newman, that St. George of the English language, was there, and a lot of people were willing to swear that his presence alone was great; Christopher Reeve, the star of *Superman*, was there, and many of the people at the party looked at him as if they

thought he was great; Gloria Swanson, the great former Hollywood beauty and actress, was there, and she was wondering
out loud if her new book—her autobiography—started too
slow to grab the reader's attention, but a woman who had just
said to her, "Miss Swanson, you don't remember me. Barbara
Walters brought me up to your apartment the other day," now
said, "Oh, but I think your book is so wonderful, so great";
Barbara Howar, the well-known Washington social person
and writer, was there, and she is extremely great; a woman
was there who was talking about that great best-seller about
that titan of society and fashion Gloria Vanderbilt, and she
was saying to a man whose greatness wasn't obvious but
couldn't be doubted, "Everything is great. The book is being
used at Harvard, Yale, and Dartmouth for the sense of history"; Dan Green, the head of one of Simon & Schuster's
great divisions, was there, and he was talking to Dominique
Lapierre, the co-author of a fictional book about New York
City being held hostage by terrorists who have an atom
bomb—which is an idea so great that most people can hardly
get through the day for worrying about it; Joni Evans, head of
her own book-publishing division under the Simon & Schuster imprint and the wife of Richard E. Snyder, was there,
and she is such a great human being that she kept trying to
get a reporter to take home some of the food that the great
guests hadn't consumed; and, of course, Merv Griffin was
there, and he shook hands with the guests and smiled at
them, and when he smiled his teeth looked white and gleam-
ing and great.

Years ago, on *The Merv Griffin Show*, the actor Forrest
Tucker, who was a guest on the show that day, turned to the
actor Mickey Rooney, who was also a guest on the show that
day, to tell him what a great actor he was. He said, "They can
put you up there with anybody. I don't care. You're greater
than any of them. You're greater than Gielgud."

—*October 20, 1980*

Romance

❦

Harlequin Books, the publishers of Harlequin Romances, recently gave a luncheon for two hundred women readers of Harlequin Romances in the large dining room of a large hotel in New Jersey. The women, each of whom looked freshly coiffed, sat at tables in the middle of which were large bowls of yellow and gold chrysanthemums. The women seemed very excited. Ahead of them: a chat by the director of consumer relations for Harlequin, a chat by a vice-president of Harlequin, a chat by a new writer of Harlequin Romances, a "bridal" bouquet to be tossed into the roomful of women by the vice-president, the cutting of a cake baked in the shape of an open book.

"I watch the Phil Donahue show when I can," said Grace to her friend Dolly. "But mostly I like to read."

"I like to read, too," said Dolly. "TV is too explicit."

"I like to read, too," said Maralyn, a friend of Dolly's but not such a good friend of Grace's. "But I don't like things to be explicit. I like an innocent girl."

"I like an innocent girl, too," said Gertrude, a very good friend of Maralyn's, though she hardly knew Grace or Dolly. "But I don't like a Barbara Cartland type of girl. They are way to the right."

"I send my children out the door," said Nora, the best friend of Gertrude and a very good friend of Maralyn's. "I do my housework, then I make myself a sandwich and curl up with one of my romances."

"A lot of men object to women reading this kind of book when they are alone," said Joanne, a good friend of none of the women sitting at the table with her. "But I say it's better than getting into mischief."

"According to a poll taken among you women," said the director of consumer relations, standing on a dais and speaking to the room at large with the help of a microphone, "the most romantic man in America is Robert Redford. The second most romantic man is 'My Husband.'"

"Hi," said the vice-president, standing on a dais and speaking to the room at large with the help of a microphone.

"Hi," said the new writer of Harlequin Romances. "They say writing is a lonely business, but I don't feel so lonely now. This is so nice! I have not been to a party like this before, and after years of being chained to the typewriter it is nice to get out and meet some real-life readers."

"That was delightful," said the vice-president to the new writer. Then, turning to the women, he said, "The first person to ask a question from each table gets the centerpiece from her table."

"Why are the men in Harlequin Romances always six feet tall and virile and in their forties and the women small and thin and seventeen?" asked a woman seated at a table in the back of the room.

"Ha, ha, ha, ha," laughed the vice-president.

"How do you get the authors to write only a certain number of pages?" asked another woman.

"Sometimes the type is larger, sometimes the type is smaller," said the vice-president. "We don't like to cut out an author's beautiful words."

Then everybody sat down and ate a lunch of salad, baked chicken, potato puffs, and baked broccoli with bread crumbs. The food wasn't very good, but nobody said so.

—November 3, 1980

Novel

✦❖✦

Oriana Fallaci, the internationally famous Italian journalist and interviewer of the high, mighty, and unbelievably important, has written and had published a novel, and to publicize it she asked eighteen people, some of whom she didn't know at all personally but all of whom she knew worked for newspapers or magazines or television, to lunch at "21." Oriana Fallaci's novel, titled *A Man*, is about a hero of the Greek resistance who uncovers evidence of great corruption and all-around wrongdoing in powerful circles in Greek politics but is killed before he can expose the wicked people. In real life, Oriana Fallaci said to her guests, she was in love with a hero of the Greek resistance who uncovered evidence of great corruption and all-around wrongdoing in powerful circles in Greek politics but was killed before he could expose the wicked people.

At the lunch, Oriana Fallaci, who is petite and pretty, sat with all her guests at an oblong dining table. A few times, she

said "you Americans" in a way that many Western Europeans
like to say "you Americans"—a way that many Americans find
annoying. She also said, "What is fiction?" and "People ask me
if this or that incident in the book was true, and I say, 'It's all
true,' though, of course, the truth is always longer." She said,
"I love politics. There are some people who don't resist alco-
hol, some people who don't resist drugs. I don't resist politics,"
and "My father laughed a lot. Once, I said to him, 'Father,
how come you always laugh and never cry?' and he said, 'It's
the same thing,'" and "You don't steel yourself against life as I
did for three years to write a book; you write it and face the
task of writing it," and "Alekos said to me, 'I will die and you
will love me forever and you'll write a book about me,'" and
"Anything can be said about me but not that I don't write
good Italian. I am Florentine, God damn it."

A guest said to her, "Oriana, journalism is something you
are in temporary retreat from."

Another guest said, "You must find Ronald Reagan interesting."

—*December 8, 1980*

Cat Story

Pussy cat, pussy cat, where have you been?
I've been to London to look at the Queen.
Pussy cat, pussy cat, what did you there?
I frightened a little mouse under her chair.

Morris, who is a cat and is (so to speak) the star of a cat-food advertising campaign, has edited (so to speak again) a book about cats and how to take care of them. Morris, who is an orange tabby cat, and his trainer, a man with a severe crew-cut, came to the city the other day to promote the book, so they invited people to come to Sardi's and ask questions and take pictures. Morris was placed on a table at one end of the room for all to see, and he licked his paws, rested his chin on his paws, half closed his eyes, moved one of his ears, moved both of his ears, lay down on his stomach, flicked his tail, and jumped off the table and tried to run away a few times.

"Is he drugged?" asked a woman, who later said that she is

very concerned about the treatment of cats in public life, is against cat shows, has five cats, and takes her cats to a cat dentist regularly.

"No," said someone connected with Morris and his trainer. "People always ask that. But Morris doesn't have to be drugged. He's a real professional."

"But isn't Morris dead?" asked another woman.

"Well, yes, but that was the other Morris," answered the connection. "It's like a dynasty. Morris is dead. Long live Morris. This Morris was found in a cat shelter. He was a stray. This is the Morris that is now used in all the ads. But there are three more in reserve, in case he should suddenly drop dead."

A grown man in a Kool-Aid-orange-and-white cat suit walked by. On his stomach, written in black letters, were the words "Personal Ambassador to Morris the Cat."

"He looks highly flammable," said a man.

"It's rough," said a woman.

Morris left the room, presumably to eat a meal of fish, fish by-products, water, crab, shrimp, animal fat, wheat flour, dried yeast, dried whey, iron oxide, vitamin E, A, and niacin supplements, thiamin mononitrate, ethylenediamine dihydroiodide, calcium pantothenate, riboflavin supplement, vitamin D_3 supplement, and pyridoxine hydrochloride, which make up the contents of a six-and-a-half-ounce can of the brand of cat food that Morris represents.

—December 15, 1980

The Exercise

PART ONE: It was noon, it was in the Terrace Room of the Plaza Hotel, there was Chris Evert Lloyd, the world-class women's tennis champion, there were some executives of an Italian sportswear company who had just flown in from Italy, there were lots of sports reporters from the electronic and print media, there was food (a buffet of beef bourguignonne, seafood crêpes, shrimps, rice, cold stringbeans, asparagus in prosciutto, and various French-related desserts), there were some tables, round, with white tablecloths, and on these tables there were some half-dead yellow mums.

"Chris," a man said.

"Hi," Chris said.

"I am sure these questions will be rather redundant to you," said a newswoman. "But I am going to ask them anyway."

"Will this five-year-exclusive contract interfere with your career?" a man asked.

"I am not doing much," Chris answered.

"Do you foresee gradual retirement?" a man asked.

"I envision a family one day," Chris answered.

"What were the factors involved in this decision for your career?" a man asked.

"How do you feel about Tracy Austin?" a woman asked.

"It's an Italian company," Chris said. "I think those Italians really know what they are doing. I really have a good feel for things."

A large, middle-aged, overweight man who had lost most of the hair on his head but had a nice bushy mustache played with the ends of his mustache as he asked the bartender for a Bloody Mary. Then, turning to his friends, four men who looked more or less like him, he said, "I think Oakland will beat the Giants." Then he reached into a bowl that was filled with salted nuts and, taking a handful, put them all into his mouth at once.

A man—a man not referred to above—went up to a lectern and said a few words about welcome, sportswear, a sportswear company, and Chris Evert Lloyd, in Italian-accented English. Another man—a man also not referred to above—then joined him and said more words about welcome, a sportswear company, and Chris Evert Lloyd, in Italian, and the other man translated what he said into Italian-accented English.

Chris Evert Lloyd then joined the two men at the lectern. One of them gave her a dozen red roses. "I am really excited about wearing Ellesse clothes, because they are really beautiful," she said. "I don't know if you've seen the line. They're

No. 1 in Europe, and I hope they'll be No. 1 in the U.S. It's the best. It deserves to be the best."

PART TWO: After reading the above, can you tell (a) that Chris Evert Lloyd, the world-class women's tennis champion, has just endorsed a line of sportswear manufactured by an Italian sportswear manufacturer? (b) how Chris Evert Lloyd feels about Tracy Austin? (c) whether most Italians speak English with an Italian accent or don't speak English at all? (d) if, according to United States government statistics, the large, middle-aged, overweight man will have a health problem soon? (e) if Chris Evert Lloyd can have visions? (f) what Chris Evert Lloyd means when she says, "I have a really good feel for things"? (g) if Chris Evert Lloyd trusts only Italian sportswear manufacturers, and not the average Italian walking down a street in Milan?

Would you have liked Chris Evert Lloyd more or less if she had been a geophysicist, a water tower, or an elephant hunted mercilessly for its valuable ivory tusks?

After reading the first paragraph, did you say to yourself, quietly or out loud, "Gee, wish I'd been there"?

If you were offered a large amount of money, would you refuse to endorse sportswear made in Italy?

If you were offered a large amount of money, would you refuse to endorse *anything*?

—*January 12, 1981*

Car Questions

> I'm a career girl in a man's world.
> I'm a career girl and I can make my own way.
>
> Go ahead baby, do your thing
> Go ahead baby, do your thing.
> —"Career Girl," by Carrie Lucas

The Ford automobile heiresses Anne and Charlotte Ford have written a book about motorcars (though only Ford cars are featured in the drawings and photographs in the book), called *How to Love the Car in Your Life*. The book, which they wrote with the assistance of two professional writers, has fifty-nine pages and is unquestionably useful. It tells the reader what to do about backseat drivers, seating arrangements, conversation in the car, neatness, smoking, eating in the car, cats and dogs in the car, buying gasoline, opening the door for a woman, getting directions, travelling with children, entering the freeway, pulling off the road. But perhaps the most useful thing about it is that it is a guide to what to say to Anne or Charlotte Ford at a party.

Guest to Anne or Charlotte Ford: "What is an automatic transaxle?"

Anne or Charlotte Ford to guest: "An automatic transaxle makes automatic shifting available in small front-wheel-drive cars equipped with transaxles."

Guest to Anne or Charlotte Ford: "What is a dipstick?"

Anne or Charlotte Ford to guest: "A thin metal rod used to check an engine's oil level."

Guest to Anne or Charlotte Ford: "What is a jack?"

Anne or Charlotte Ford to guest: "If you don't want to be your own demolition derby, it's important to know that proper positioning of the jack varies from car to car."

The other day, the people at the Ford Motor Company threw a cocktail party for Anne and Charlotte Ford at the new Palace Hotel. Almost all the guests there looked as though they never drove themselves anywhere, or, if they did, they didn't actually have to. Anne, who studies political science at the New School, wore a short, snazzy-looking black dress. Charlotte, an acclaimed designer of women's clothing and the author of a book on etiquette, also wore a short, snazzy-looking black dress. Governor Carey was there, and as he stood between Anne and Charlotte Ford and posed for photographers he looked less like a governor, though not like a mayor. Former Mayor Wagner was there, and he looked like a mayor and a governor and a President all rolled into one.

Anne and Charlotte Ford's children were there, and they were very friendly. Anne Ford's piano teacher was there, and he was very nice and said a lot of nice things about her. About Charlotte Ford we heard a woman who is in the public-relations department of the Ford Motor Company say to the Ford account executive at the Wells, Rich, Greene ad agency, "Only you would appreciate this story of one-upmanship. The other day, I was up at Charlotte's apartment and we were going over the guest list. She came to Mary Wells' name and she said, 'My God! I've never met Mary Wells Lawrence.' And so I said, 'Well, I have, ha, ha, ha.' Of course, you know Charlotte is very interested in women who make it on their own, and for that Mary Wells is the ultimate role model."

—January 19, 1981

Tableware

Just before she left the house the other morning, said Letitia Baldridge, who has revised and expanded *The Amy Vanderbilt Complete Book of Etiquette,* to a roomful of tableware manufacturers and merchandisers, her husband said to her, "My God! Who would want to hear you at this hour?" Miss Baldridge, a large, pink-faced woman, said this with such comic skill that the whole roomful of tableware manufacturers and merchandisers laughed extremely hard. Miss Baldridge told them that she went to Vassar, and received a B.A., but the funny thing about going to college was that when she graduated she couldn't type, she couldn't take shorthand, and she couldn't file. The roomful of tableware manufacturers and merchandisers let that pass. Then, said Miss Baldridge, she went to work for Ambassador David Bruce and his wife, Evangeline, at the United States Embassy in Paris. Evangeline Bruce, she said, was an incredible woman, who could speak seven languages by the time she was seventeen, cared very much about how a table looked, and would always take care of the table setting herself. But then once, for some reason or other, Miss Baldridge had to take care of the table setting all by herself. At this particular dinner, there were more men than women, so some of the men had to be seated next to each other. Well, when they all sat down, it turned out that Miss Baldridge had seated one of the top ambassadors next to his wife's lover, and, because the ambassador and his wife and his wife's lover were an open secret, everybody at the dinner almost passed out. And so did the roomful of tableware manufacturers and merchandisers; again they laughed extremely hard. When something like this happens, she said, you don't cry about it, because then it only gets worse. After that, she told about working for Ambassadress Clare Boothe Luce, in Italy. This was soon after the Second World War, and what an experience *that* was! The Italians were so baroque, the dollar was tops, and the Luces were wonderful. Miss Baldridge, on the other hand, had her problems. There was the time she introduced the Pakistani Ambassador to a party of Italians as the Indian Ambassador. That didn't go down too well with the Pakistani Ambassador, naturally, but it got a big laugh from the roomful of tableware manufacturers and merchandisers. And the time when, for the first dinner she organized, everything was white—everything: the dishes, the soup, the wine. It wasn't funny then, but it got a big laugh now. And the time she served some Mormons a dinner they couldn't eat: the soup had sherry in it, and the fish had been cooked in white wine, the meat in red wine, the dessert in cognac. It wasn't funny then, but it was sidesplitting now. Winding up, Miss Baldridge told about working for Tiffany's, and how once, for a display, she ordered some exotic birds, and how they escaped from their cage, causing near-havoc on the third floor, which was filled with fine crystal and china. For that, the roomful of tableware manufacturers and merchandisers had lots of sharp intakes of breath. Miss Baldridge told about working in the White House for Mrs. Jacqueline Kennedy, and what a great decorator and restorer Mrs. Kennedy was, and how conscious of the tableware she was. The roomful of tableware manufacturers and merchandisers emitted some "Ah!"s. Then Miss Baldridge said that it was a wonderful world and an affirmative world, and the roomful of tableware manufacturers and merchandisers applauded wildly, as if they were surprised and grateful that someone could feel that way after a life filled with table settings.

—*January 26, 1981*

Prince

✦

Late one afternoon, the Crown Prince of Benin, his uncle, an anthropology professor named Flora S. Kaplan, some men who are associated in one way or another with the Royal Court of Benin, some American men who are associated in one way or another with foundation endowments and grants, a still photographer, and a motion-picture photographer went to the Grey Art Gallery at New York University to see an exhibit of art objects from the Royal Court of Benin. The art objects, which are extremely beautiful, are now owned by people none of whom are African.

(Information, taken mostly from the press release that came in the mail: Benin today is the capital of Bendel State, in the Federal Republic of Nigeria; it is a city reposing in a high tropical rain forest eighty miles west of the Niger River. In precolonial times, Benin was the political and cultural center of a vast kingdom known as Benin, which flourished from the thirteenth century until the British Punitive Expedition of

1897; the present Benin is to be distinguished from the People's Republic of Benin, which used to be called Dahomey, and which borders Nigeria on the west. The Benin monarchy has continued in an unbroken line of descent for over five hundred and fifty years, and a new *Oba*, or Divine King, was installed in 1979. Many of Benin's historical rituals are still observed.)

The visit went something like this: Dr. Kaplan, who was responsible for the exhibit in the first place and so was officiating more as a hostess than as an anthropology professor, gathered around her the Crown Prince, his uncle, the men of the Benin court, and the men of the endowments and grants, so that they could all have their picture taken. Dr. Kaplan, who seemed notably energetic and notably eager, said to the Crown Prince, "There has never been a museum exhibition of this kind in New York, but I wanted to make people in this country aware of the culture and history of Benin. Many people in this country don't have a sense of geography or history. To us, history is two years old. Since Nigeria is so important to us, since Africa is so important to us, I really felt we should make this contribution."

The Crown Prince, who had said that he was a graduate of the University of Wales, and that he was in the United States to acquire knowledge and to broaden his horizon, nodded vigorously at Dr. Kaplan.

The Crown Prince then walked around the room. He said that as a boy he was always being reminded of who he was, that he was never allowed to go about alone, that he was never allowed to eat food outside his home or food that his family had not prepared for him, and that he was always being told whom to see and whom not to see. Everyone listened to him as he talked.

Then one of the endowments-and-grants men asked, "What is the distance from Benin to Lagos?"

"Seven hours' drive," the Crown Prince answered.

"What direction?" the same man asked.

"West," the Crown Prince answered.

"I am trying to place in my own mind the Kingdom of Benin in Nigerian life," said the man.

"Benin existed before Nigeria," said the Crown Prince.

"It's a hairline, isn't it—a delicate balance between the old and the new?" said the man.

"Yes," said the Crown Prince.

Dr. Kaplan, who had left the Crown Prince and the other men for a moment, now rejoined them. She looked around her, then turned to the Crown Prince, smiled, and said, "It must be an interesting feeling to come in here and see so much of home."

"Ha, ha, ha, yes," laughed and said the Crown Prince.

—*April 20, 1981*

Notes and Comment

Early this year, a Frenchman commandeered a helicopter and ordered it flown to a prison outside Paris, where he helped two friends, who were inmates at the time, escape. A few days later, one of the inmates was captured. Recently, the two other men were caught, hiding out in Spain. We saw a report of this on television with a friend. Our friend said, "Wow, that was so daring I am all for it." We could see what he meant. We could see it so clearly that we have made a list of our own of things that are so daring—well . . .

Instead of adding books to school libraries, removing books from school libraries: so daring I'm all for it.

A Secretary of the Interior who actually hates the interior: so daring I'm all for it.

Someone who is against a human-rights policy chosen to be in charge of our human-rights policy: so daring I'm all for it.

Phil Donahue: so daring I'm all for it.

Mayor Koch: so daring I'm all for it.

Reviving the HUAC: so daring I'm all for it.

Abandoning the Voting Rights Act: so daring I'm all for it.

Revoking the Clean Air Act: so daring I'm all for it.

Suing your parents: so daring I'm all for it.

Writing a book in which you reveal sensational and shameful details of your personal life: so daring I'm all for it.

Tearing down a beautiful old building and putting in its place an ugly new building: so daring I'm all for it.

The arms race: so daring I'm all for it.

World War III: so daring I'm all for it.

—July 27, 1981

The Apprentice

A woman we know who takes a deep interest in clothes and the fabrics that they are made up in, and who, it seems, occasionally makes herself a dress or a pair of trousers or a blouse, invited us to go "look at some cloth," as she put it. On our way, she said, "On the day I turned seven, my mother gave me a copy of the *Concise Oxford Dictionary*, and in it she wrote, 'To my darling daughter, with love, Mamie.' And also she said, 'Miss Doreen can take you now.' Miss Doreen was a seamstress. She wasn't my seamstress and she wasn't my mother's seamstress, though sometimes she was asked to make my everyday school uniform. What my mother meant by her taking me now was that I could begin to be her new apprentice. We lived on a small island in the Caribbean, and everyone I knew then was apprenticing to someone—the girls to cooks or seamstresses or housekeepers, the boys to carpenters or mechanics or men busy at some other thing that men do. My father was a carpenter, and some boy's mother was always at our house asking if the boy could become my father's apprentice. My father's apprentice had to carry my father's toolbox and walk behind my father, and he couldn't stop and talk to people while he was with my father. At the time I began with Miss Doreen, I already knew how to sew on a button, and how to sew two things together, using a simple in-and-out stitch. But that made no difference to her. This is what she had me do: for the first few months, at the end of every sewing day it was my job to sweep up the floors, which were always covered with threads and scraps of cloth; I dusted her sewing machine; and at the end of every week I polished its mahogany cabinet. It was almost a year before I could tie off the ends of threads on the wrong side of a dress, and then only if it was a child's everyday dress. It was years before I was allowed to go to the store with a sample of cloth and buy the matching-color thread for it. I was fourteen years old before I was asked to hem a woman's Sunday dress. In between all these things, though, she showed me how to make buttonholes, how to cut on the bias, how to make a gathered skirt, how to make pleats. When she worked, she would purse her lips; and she was very bony—her collarbones really stuck out. I would go to see her on Tuesdays and Thursdays from four to six when I had school, and from one o'clock to three o'clock three days a week during school holidays. I never saw her on weekends. She was a Seventh Day Adventist. She charged five shillings to make a woman's dress and two shillings and sixpence to make a child's dress. I haven't seen her in years. I don't know what it is she does now. I don't know if she is dead or alive."

At the fabric store, a large, barnlike room filled with rows and rows of bolts of cloth stacked on top of each other in a disorderly way, our friend said, "It's all been changed since I was here last. They used to keep linen here." She pointed to a place where there were bolts of silky-looking material. "I haven't been here in years, so everything must have changed. There used to be a man who worked here—I liked him. He was always so nice to me. He would always go in the back and bring me some piece of fabric that he thought I would like. Once, he showed me the most beautiful piece of French silk crêpe. It was pink with large blue flowers. I used to like to stand and watch him cut the cloth. He had little tufts of hair growing in his ears. Of course, the thing about this place is that you can find wonderful fabric, and none of it is too dear. Now I shall just walk by and look."

Our friend walked along the aisles. She tugged at and shuffled between her fingers taffeta, silk, organza, wool, cotton, crêpe de Chine, gabardine, wool challis. She held some of these fabrics up against her body, and she seemed on the verge of buying yards of red and pink plain cotton. She said, "None of this is really right. It's none of it exactly what I want. I know just what I want. Or I will know it when I see it. What I guess I really want is some handkerchief linen. But they don't have any handkerchief linen here. Usually, it costs fifteen dollars a yard. They have some nice gingham. I like gingham a lot, though only in a certain way. When I was little, I had many dresses made up in gingham. Some of them were decorated with braid and some of them with smocking. At my school, the girls were allowed to wear dresses on Fridays. Also on Fridays, the person who was the best student for the week would receive from the teacher a small prize. It might be a two-tone rubber eraser or a special notebook, made in France. For a long time, almost every week I was the best student. If I wasn't the best student, I was the second-best student, but usually I was the best. This made some other girls annoyed at me, and on one Friday afternoon, when I went into the bathroom, they came with me. Then they picked me up and tried to flush me away. Feet first, thank God. On that day, I was wearing one of my gingham dresses."

—*August 17, 1981*

Meeting

One evening recently:

In the ballroom (an ordinary-looking ballroom, with large star-bursting-up-shaped lamps hanging from the ceiling) of the new Vista International New York Hotel (situated at the World Trade Center, and the newest United States hotel in the chain of Hilton International Hotels), there were two hundred and eighty people, most of them the managers of Hilton hotels and their wives, and then there was Catherine Tritsch, the managing editor of *Successful Meetings*, which is a magazine for corporation and association people who plan meetings. The Hilton managers and their wives had spent the last few days meeting each other in a business-conference way and meeting each other over meals. Now, in the ballroom, they were meeting to eat a dinner of clam chowder, steamed clams, boiled lobster, boiled ears of corn, and watermelon.

Catherine Tritsch, the managing editor of *Successful Meet-*

ings, said to us, "People think that the people who go to conventions don't eat well. The theory is that they are rubes, they don't know good food. But it's not true. People who go to conventions are high-income people, and they are very professional."

The Woody Herman orchestra was there, and it was led by Woody Herman himself, and it played some songs, all of them popular old American songs. "A good convention banquet will create the atmosphere of a good restaurant," said Catherine Tritsch. "A good restaurant has to have a theme. This has a theme. American food. American music."

There was a waitress wearing knicker-style pants and there was a waitress who looked more or less like a colonial maiden, but all the rest of the people who were waiting on the tables were waiters, and there was no mistaking them.

"Did you know that waiters who serve at banquets have their own union?" Catherine Tritsch asked us. "If you have so many people, you have to have so many waiters. Union rules."

A man got up from his table and, taking up a small American flag, led a number of people halfway around the ballroom. Then he came back to his own table, and he and the men sitting with him tied their napkins around their heads as if they were pirates.

"These people are upscale people," said Catherine Tritsch. "High-income people. Very cosmopolitan. This is a successful meeting."

Among them, Catherine Tritsch and the two hundred and eighty other people, most of whom were hotel managers and their wives, ate and drank eighteen gallons of clam chowder, three hundred lobsters, three thousand clams, four hundred ears of corn, fifteen cases of wine, seven barrels of beer, and sixty watermelons.

—September 14, 1981

Birthday Party at an East Side Town House

"Hello, I am so glad you could come," said Gwendolyn, the assistant editor of a literary magazine, greeting some of the guests at her twenty-sixth-birthday party. As she said this, she kissed each of them on the cheek. There were well over a hundred guests at the party. They all knew Gwendolyn and said how glad they were to come.

Now she stood in the middle of the room surrounded by these friends, who were momentarily and randomly grouped together. A young man joined the group.

"Do you know Tommy?" Gwendolyn asked her friends. "We grew up in Virginia together. His father and my father went to all the same schools."

"Tommy," said a friend standing beside her, a man named George.

"Tommy," murmured the others.

"I am so honored that Victor came," she said. "He does my hair. He is a wonderful man."

"Victor," said George.

"Victor," murmured the others.

"That tree is too large for this room," said a man named Maurice, pointing to a plant that if it stood in a forest would be a mere sapling.

"But isn't this a beautiful room?" asked Gwendolyn.

"I think *you* are beautiful," said a man named Chris.

"Natalia writes beautifully about food," said Maurice.

"Food," said Tommy.

"A drink," said George.

"Maurice has almost finished writing his book," said Gwendolyn.

"I am trying not to mention it," said Maurice.

"Have you received many presents?" asked Chris.

"Yes, but I am not opening them until tomorrow," said Gwendolyn.

"I am giving you a book," said Chris. "I am giving you a book full of pictures."

"Oh," said Gwendolyn. "What kind of pictures?"

"They are the most beautiful pictures I have ever seen," said Chris. "I have been looking at these pictures for months and months now, day after day."

"Will I like them?" asked Gwendolyn.

"Yes, I think so," said Chris. "I look at these pictures and I am emptied out. I have nothing left inside once I have seen these pictures. I feel so much when I am looking at them. Lots and lots of sensation, and then I am drained. It's as if I had been in Los Angeles. Sensation, as you know, is the tyranny of Los Angeles."

"A book of pictures," said Gwendolyn.

"A book of pictures," murmured her friends.

—May 10, 1982

Foam and Brass

❧✦❧

Early one morning, we went up to the National Academy of Design, on Fifth Avenue, to view a number of objects, some of a utilitarian nature, some of an aesthetic nature, that were all made of something called Prime-Foam-X. Prime-Foam-X is in fact the clay-coated paper-and-foam backing used for mounting photographs. The clay-coated paper-and-foam backing used for mounting photographs was first put on the market by the Monsanto Company, which called it Fome-Cor. Its generic name is foam board. Almost everybody who uses a clay-coated paper-and-foam backing, however, calls it Fome-Cor, the way almost everybody who has a cold uses Kleenex, and not tissue. The makers of Prime-Foam-X may have thought it unfortunate that the Monsanto product has always been No. 1 in the foam-board market. In any case, they decided to have a contest. They invited people to make objects from their product.

At the exhibit, we were met by a woman representative of

the Prime-Foam-X company—the Primex Plastics Corporation—and she showed us around. We saw a skeleton of a dinosaur with its head lowered, as if the flesh had been stripped
away while it fed. We saw something that was said to be a
Relativity Chronolith and seemed to have something to do
with the Mayan Indians. We saw *Portrait of Miss Bowles*, a
print of a painting by Sir Joshua Reynolds, in a frame that was
made from Prime-Foam-X but attempted to look like mahogany. We saw a large cutout of a man with a blue coat, gray
trousers, and a yellow-and-gray tie; his special significance
was never clear to us. We saw a game that was so new it had
not been patented yet. We saw a chair, hand-carved in the
Queen Anne style, but we were warned that it could not
support a grownup human body. We saw a portable desk, la-
belled "Calligrapher's Desk." We saw a doll-sized round
house, with unreal potted plants inside it and framed paint-
ings on the walls. We saw a collapsible lamp. We saw a
present-day sports car. We saw a sports car that was said to
belong in the future.

Our guide now said that perhaps we would like to see the
helicopter, which was being housed in the church next door,
it being too big for the Design building. She said, "You cannot
imagine the remarkable versatility of this product. The as-
tounding thing is that no one ever thought you could do all
this with a piece of foam." We walked over to the church, and
saw something that looked like a helicopter in a highly imagi-
native school pageant. For one thing, the frame was made
from the frame of an old wicker wheelchair—stripped of its

wicker. Our guide pointed to the person who had made the helicopter. It was a man, and he wore black trousers and a black tunic covered with concave mirrors—an important part of the Polaroid SX-70 Land camera.

At noon, we went down to "21," where Phelps Dodge Industries was giving a lunch to introduce some expensive decorative household wares, all made out of brass. They are done in something called the Federal Period, and they are a wine cooler, a basket suitable for holding fruit, a bowl suitable for holding fruit, a tray, a compote dish, and a plate. Many of the guests looked at them, and many of the guests thought them beautiful. After the lunch, which many of the guests said was delicious, a man, an executive of Phelps Dodge Industries, made a speech. He said that people had thought his company audacious, impudent, and foolhardy to go into the consumer business. He mentioned someone who had been orphaned at age eleven and had apprenticed himself to a saddlemaker. He said that brass was a hot item. He said that the competition was foreign and its products were generally of a poor quality. He said that there was no real standard for brass. He said that there was little evidence of professional design in brass products. He said that eighty-five per cent of all brass products are purchased by women. He said that some people found brass too yellow. He said that his company was the No. 2 producer of copper in this country. He seemed to have no doubt that this new venture would be a big success.

—*July 12, 1982*

Knitting

꧁❖꧂

There is a store called the Country Store & Yarn Shop in the small town of Washington, Connecticut, where one can buy all sorts of materials and instruments used in handicrafts, and especially in knitting. It is perhaps the nicest store in the world, because it is run and owned by perhaps one of the nicest women in the world—a woman named Beatrice Morse Davenport, or Bea to almost everybody who comes into the store. Mrs. Davenport, a gentle-looking, shy, grandmotherly woman, still has the gait of a girl who is afraid she'll be judged too tall, and she peers at objects and people from behind her glasses, her head tilted to one side, in the odd, calm way of someone who makes things with her hands. Mrs. Davenport is quite accomplished in all the needlecrafts, but she is an exceptional knitter, and it is knitting problems, a wish for knitting instruction, and the purchasing of yarns and needles that bring most people to her store. She seems happy to help solve problems, gives instruction free of charge, and offers sound advice on the purchasing of yarns and needles. We visited her in her store the other day, and while she was correcting a mistake made in an enormous afghan by a friend of ours (some stitches dropped four rows down, Mrs. Davenport had told our friend, adding that to unravel the afghan, which was about four yards wide, would mean losing many hours of work) she said these things to us:

"My mother taught me to knit when I was about nine years old. I used to knit all my dolls' clothes. Then I picked up things here and there and I got to be better than my mother. I had to show her how to follow a pattern. I think I made myself a sweater when I was sixteen, and then I just stopped until my first child was coming. Well, you know, if you are going to have a baby you have to make a nice baby sweater. Somebody saw the sweater I made, and wanted one like it, and so I made another sweater, and then somebody at the New York Exchange for Woman's Work saw it and asked me to knit for them. I knitted things for the Exchange for twelve years. I stopped because I had too many other orders to fill. By that time, I was knitting for designers in New York. I knitted for a woman named Jane von Schreiber. That was in the forties. Few people know who she is today, but in those days she was quite big. Margaret Sommerfeld is another person I knitted for. And somebody named Margaret Macy. I don't remember if I ever saw her. They would just send me a sketch of whatever it was they wanted, and I would make it. I did all this at home while my children were growing up, because I wanted to be with them. When Walt, my son, was ready for college, I began selling yarn. Then, when they were all off at college, I bought a store. My first store was a part of what's now the Washington Food Market, here in Washington.

"Right away, I started selling Irish yarn. I imported the yarns myself from Ireland, because the yarn companies hadn't picked up on Irish yarns yet. People would buy the yarn, but then they would want a pattern to make the yarn into something, so I would just make up a pattern for them. I love to knit so much. If you really want to know, I started to knit for people because my children had all the sweaters they could wear, and by that time I just had to keep knitting, and so I did. The whole thing excites me so much. When I see a new yarn, I think, Oh, I know what should be done with that. It's terrible to be so enthusiastic at my age, isn't it? But it gives me so much satisfaction. I just got a letter from a woman in England telling me about a sweater I had made for her little sister years and years ago. Her sister wore the sweater, and then I guess it was put away, because the sister's four children all wore it at one time or another, and now this woman's son, a cousin of the four children, is wearing it. I had forgotten what it looked like, so she sent me a picture of the little boy wearing it. Now, that's satisfying."

Mrs. Davenport studied the afghan, with all the stitches picked up and correctly in place, and then she looked up and smiled. "There," she said.

—*July 12, 1982*

Notes and Comment

A young woman writes:

The carpenter is at my house replacing the frames and glass panes of some windows. She (it is a woman, a round, fair woman who looks more like a cook than like a carpenter, but she is a good carpenter, as I soon see) has around her strips of wood, panes of glass, a glass cutter, a large portable electric saw, nails, hammers, and something called a caulk gun. She measures, she saws, she cuts, she sighs: it is a much more complicated job than she at first thought, the house being a very old and crooked house. The work is taking place in a bedroom, and I sit on the edge of a bed all the time, watching her. There are many things for me to do around the house; I should also go out and run some errands. But I cannot leave the carpenter's presence. Perhaps I will be able to assist in some way; perhaps she will say something to me.

My father was a carpenter, and a cabinetmaker, too. In the world (and it was a small world: a hundred and eight square miles, a population of sixty thousand, no deep-water harbor, so large ships had to anchor way offshore), my father was the second-best carpenter and cabinetmaker. The best carpenter was Mr. Walters, to whom my father had been apprenticed as a boy and for whom he had worked when he was a young man. Mr. Walters had been dead for a long time, even before I was born, but he was still the best carpenter and cabinetmaker. My father was so devoted to this man that he did everything just the way Mr. Walters would have done it. If, for instance, in 1955 you asked my father to build you a house and make you some simple chair to sit on in it, he would build you a house and make you a chair exactly like the house and the chair Mr. Walters would have built in 1915.

My father left our house for work every weekday morning at seven o'clock, by the striking of the Anglican church bell. If it was his first day on a new job, one of his apprentices would come by a little before seven o'clock to pick up my father's toolbox. If it was one of the older apprentices, he could walk along with my father, and they might talk. If it was one of the younger boys, he would have to walk a few steps behind. At around four o'clock in the afternoon, my father returned home. If he saw me then, he would say, "Well, we got everything in place today." And I would say, in reply, "Oh, sir, that's very good." After that, he would disappear into his shop, where he made furniture.

In my father's shop, everything was some shade of brown. First, there was the color of his skin; and he wore khaki trousers and khaki shirts, brown shoes, and a brown felt hat.

He smoked cigarettes (Lucky Strikes) one after another, and he smoked so much that the thumb and the index and middle fingers of his right hand were stained brown. His hands were stained another shade of brown from handling stained wood, wood oils, and glues. Everything was brown, that is, except the red, flat carpenter's pencil (such an unusual, distinctive shape for a pencil, I thought, and I was sadly disappointed when I discovered that it was not a good writing pencil) that he carried perched always behind his right ear. Sometimes when I went to watch him work, he would tell me little things about himself when he was a young man. He would talk about himself as if he were someone he used to know very well, someone he thought really an admirable person, someone he would like very much. Mostly, they were stories about himself as a cricketer. He never told me that he was good at playing cricket; I already knew that.

My father made very beautiful furniture. Everybody said so—especially my mother, who would then point out that unfortunately none of this furniture was in our own house. I think almost every time she saw my father make something she would say to him that it would be nice to have one like that, and he would then promise to make another one, for her specially. But he never did. Finally, one day, he told her that the reason he was reluctant to make us up lots of furniture was that the furniture in Mrs. Walters' house (the widow of the man to whom he had been apprenticed) was really his: that he had made it up for himself when he was a very young man; that he had lent it to Mrs. Walters after her husband died and she had moved into a smaller house, the house she still lived in; that he had always meant to ask for it back one day; and that he would ask her for it soon. He never, of course, asked for the furniture—I don't think he could bring himself to. My mother could not believe that we were never to have that beautiful furniture; that at Christmastime, when our friends stopped by to have a glass of rum, if too many of them came by at once some of them would always have to sit on the floor. My father would visit Mrs. Walters quite often, and every once in a while my mother would go along with him. Afterward, she would always be furious that she had had to leave what she began calling "my furniture" behind, and she would have a big row with herself, for my father never quarrelled with anyone—not even his wife. Once, my father took me with him on one of the visits. I got a good look at the furniture, and I began to understand my mother's point of view. There was a dining table with six matching cane-bottomed chairs (my father did all his own caning); there was a little round table the edge of which was scalloped; there was a table with fancy decorative carvings on its sides and, above it, a mirror in a frame with decorative carvings that matched the ones on the table; and there was a sofa, a cabinet with delicate woodworking on the glass front, and two Morris chairs. (At the time, I did not know—nor, for that matter, do I think anyone else knew—that there was someone named Morris who had made chairs of which these two were replicas.) We had nothing like any of this in our house.

Once, my father got sick, and the doctor said that it was

his heart, and gave him some medicine and told him to stay home and rest. My mother, looking up heart diseases in one of her numerous medical books, said that the sickness was from all the cigarettes he smoked. At the same time, I took sick with a case of hookworm, and my mother, looking up hookworm in one of her numerous medical books, said that it was because I had walked around barefoot behind her back, and it was true that I did that. (I was disappointed when it was discovered that I had hookworm, and not beriberi. I would have liked to say to my friends when they asked why I wasn't in school, "Oh, I have beriberi.") Since my father couldn't go to work and I couldn't go to school, we spent all day together. In the mornings, I would go and lie with him in my parents' bed. We would lie on our backs, our hands clasped behind our necks (me imitating him), and our feet up on the windowsill in the sun. We would lie there without saying a word to each other, the only sound being *pttt, pttt* from my father as he forced small pieces of tobacco from his mouth. He continued to smoke, though not as much as before. At midmorning, my mother would come in to look at us. As soon as she came into the room, she would always ask us to take our feet off the windowsill, and we would do it right away, but as soon as she left we would put them back. When she came, she would bring with her little things to eat. Sometimes it was barley water and a special porridge, made from seaweed; sometimes it was a beaten egg-yolks-and-milk drink, sweetened with powdered sugar; sometimes it was a custard of some kind. Whatever it was, she would say that it would help to build us up. Before she left, she would kiss us on our foreheads and say that we were her two invalids, the big one and the little one. In the afternoons, after our lunch, my father and I would go off to look for a wild elderberry bush and pick elderberries. He was sure that a draught prepared from the elderberries would make his heart get better faster than the medicine the doctor had prescribed. In fact, I think he took the medicine the doctor gave him only because he thought my mother might perhaps die herself if he didn't. After we had picked the elderberries, we would go and sit in the Botanical Gardens under a rubber tree. Then he would tell me stories about his own father. He had not known his father very well at all, since his father was always going off somewhere—usually somewhere in South America—to work, but he never said anything that showed he found his father at fault. Once, he said, his father had taken a boat to Panama to build the Panama Canal. The boat got caught in a storm and sank. His father was in the sea for eleven days, just barely hanging on to a raft. He was rescued by a passing ship, which took him on to Panama, where he built the Panama Canal. For a long time, I thought that my father's father had built the Panama Canal single-handed except perhaps with the help of one or two people, the way my father himself built things single-handed except with the help of one or two people.

—January 13, 1983

Luncheon

※◆※

"And just what is this particular luncheon for?" asked the man of his enthusiastic companion, the girl, as they entered a restaurant crowded with people who were holding glasses filled with liquids and ice and standing among tables already set up for dining.

"This is a luncheon for people who have been in a movie," said the girl. "There is Bruce Dern, there is Robert Mitchum, there is Martin Sheen, there is Paul Sorvino," she said in one breath and pointing with her chin.

"There is Stacy Keach," said the man, pointing with a finger.

"There is your finger falling off and lying on the floor," said the girl. "You mustn't point."

"I like the waitresses," said the man. "They favor bangs and short, blunt-cut hair; dresses above their knees; and boots that fall down to their ankles."

"Martin Sheen has just beamed at me," said the girl.

"Martin Sheen has just beamed at that nice woman standing a step or two behind you," said the man.

"Martin Sheen is not as tall as I had expected, and yet he's not short enough to be devastatingly appealing," said the girl.

"I see that we are being asked to sit down now," said the man.

"There are rolls on the table," said the girl.

"There are always rolls on the table," said the man, "and nobody seems to eat them. When I find food just sitting on the top of a table somewhere, I won't eat it before washing it."

"Have you spoken to the man who has taken a large amount of his hair from the right side of his head and brushed it all the way over to the left side, only it won't quite lie still and so as you speak to him you are constantly tempted to put it back as it was originally and at the same time straighten his tie?" asked the girl.

"I have spoken to a man who writes exclusively about tennis and who grew up in Wilkes-Barre," said the man.

"A woman has mentioned interviewing Robert Mitchum," said the girl, "and now I see him sitting over there, his lunch untouched in front of him."

"What are we eating?" asked the man.

"Chicken in lemon sauce with French fries and boiled beans," said the girl.

"I know, but what are we really eating?" asked the man.

"Bruce Dern takes each of his French fries, butters it thoroughly, and then eats it," said the girl.

"Bruce Dern has said he is the only man who has killed John Wayne," said the man.

"From where I am sitting, in my view is Stacy Keach," said the girl. "I always feel that I should like what is in my view, so I make a great effort to sit facing attractive people."

"I wish the room were aglow," said the man. "I wish I had a feeling of expansiveness and fulfillment and delight in small, unimportant things. I cannot finish my chicken."

"I have noticed," said the girl, "that whenever people want you to eat a strange sort of animal they immediately tell you that it tastes just like chicken. This chicken that you cannot finish tastes just like chicken."

—January 17, 1983

At Mr. Chow's

The invitation read, "Countess Christina Wachtmeister, Lord Jermyn, and Susan Blond invite you to a late night party in honour of Culture Club and their American triumph. Saturday, February 26. Mr. Chow's. 324 East 57th Street. 11:30 P.M. RSVP Epic Records. Present this invitation at door."

"I suppose you know the names and recognize the faces of many of the people here," said the man.

"There's a girl whose style of dressing was once described in a book on fashion and fashionable people as grouchy simplicity," said the girl.

"I suppose you know this restaurant well and eat here all the time," said the man.

"There's the rock critic Lisa Robinson, there's the photographer Sonia Moskowitz, there's the artist and personality Marja Samson, there's John Sykes, the director of programming for MTV, there's Maria Vidal, formerly of the group Desmond Child and Rouge, there's Gregg Geller, the A. & R.

man who signed the group Culture Club to the Epic label, there's Lord Jermyn, a man who is said to own the longest Mercedes in the world and who is also one of the hosts, there's the rock musician Rick Derringer, there's the rock musician Stevie Winwood, there's the English rock singer Boy George's manager, Tony Gordon," said the girl.

"Whenever I am introduced to someone, I always wonder what he or she was like as a child," said the man.

"There's a stunning black girl dressed in a long white shift," said the girl.

"Though, of course, sometimes when I am introduced to someone I wonder what he or she might be like as something other than a child, doing things other than what a child might do," said the man.

"There's another stunning black girl, with hair that stands up on end as if she were in a comic book and had just had an incredible fright," said the girl.

"Boy George is a man and yet he wears makeup and therefore sometimes looks like a woman," said the man.

"I saw Boy George walking down the street one day and to myself I admired his shade of lipstick," said the girl.

"Boy George is a white man and yet when he sings he sounds like a black girl, a very young black girl," said the man.

"That day, just before I saw Boy George walking down the street, I had been singing his song 'Do You Really Want to Hurt Me' to myself: 'Do you really want to hurt me, Do you really want to make me cry.' I thought, What a coincidence, until I saw that it was a big hit on the charts. Half the people who saw Boy George that day were singing his song shortly before. That day I saw Boy George, I thought, How bold of him to wear so much foundation on his face and not worry about clogged pores," said the girl.

"I should like to go home and sleep in my bed now," said the man. "My bed is a bed, I recognize it to be my bed, I never wonder about anything when I am lying in my bed."

—March 14, 1983